Study Hacks

Learn From the Best to Get Amazing Grades in Less Time

(The Art of Becoming a Badass Straight-a Student While Working Less)

Paula Beekman

Published By **Darby Connor**

Paula Beekman

Study Hacks: Learn From the Best to Get Amazing Grades in Less Time (The Art of Becoming a Badass Straight-a Student While Working Less)

ISBN   978-1-998901-18-0

Legal & Disclaimer

Table Of Contents

Introduction

This e-book consists of productivity hacks and strategies that will help you take a look at, observe, and keep greater of your commands correctly.

Lots of university college college students take into account that the essential aspect to effective reading is by means of way of way of taking vicinity countless marathon take a look at sessions. They have a look at subjects and instructions for hours and hours, wondering that the longer time they spend on their books and notes will help them better keep data later.

But have you ever ever ever professional some kind of statistics overload while on a take a look at marathon? Or have you ever ever had hassle remembering all of the ones instructions you've attempted to memorize and recognize with the aid of coronary heart some weeks after your study periods?

Don't worry; you're no longer by myself. Several college college students feel the brunt of being bombarded by using using loads of information, making it tough to go through in mind standards after some days or possibly weeks.

But the fine data is that you can without troubles transfer your look at fashion to a miles a lot much less time-consuming however extra powerful one. This e-book will display you techniques that lessen the time you spend collectively with your books whilst enhancing your gaining knowledge of potential in the end. Isn't it a laugh to have a look at for shorter durations of time whilst getting the most out of your schooling?

So, flow on and look at this ebook. Take your pick out and get prepared for smoother-crusing have a observe instructions at the way to finally lead you to that sweet achievement.

Chapter 1: Pre-Testing and Quizzing

Have you ever tried answering a pre-take a look at before you dive into your actual instructions? How does it experience to answer an examination on the identical time as you haven't studied something approximately it however?

And have you ever ever experienced quizzing yourself at fantastic intervals in the lesson you're reading? Of route, your teachers or professors have accomplished this lots of instances in faculty, however did you ever bear in mind quizzing yourself during your own study instructions?

Pre-assessments and quizzes are remarkable sporting activities for your thoughts. Research has examined that taking the ones tests even without previous data of the undertaking prepares you well for digesting the statistics your new lesson consists of. It additionally extensively improves retention, as evidenced through improved results in the path of placed up-exams.

This financial damage will offer an cause of the blessings of pre-attempting out and quizzing yourself. We'll moreover deal with the exceptional methods to comprise pre-attempting out and quizzing for your observe repertoire.

What Exactly Is Pre-Test and Quizzing?

Pre-exams are examinations given to students earlier than the lesson is truly taught or supplied. Quizzing, but, is answering brief questions or small tests even as the lessons are ongoing.

Both kinds of tests are considerably used by instructors and professors within the school room. However, the ones can also be used during self-have a have a look at and enterprise observe classes.

Multiple-choice questions are commonly applied in pre-tests and quizzes. This can variety, although. Other exam types which include essays, identity, and enumeration are also used depending on the subjects handy.

There are hundreds of books and reviewers with pre-tests and quizzes specifically-designed for self-compare functions. Answer keys and rationales explaining the proper answers are commonly blanketed in the ones books.

Benefits of Pre-Testing and Quizzing

Here are a number of the advantages of pre-attempting out and quizzing subsequently of a take a look at consultation:

Pre-checks are a manner to prepare you for the instructions you'll face in some time. It gives you an outline of the important topics you need to recognize about a lesson. It furthermore reinforces the dreams, desires, and expectancies of the lesson.

Pre-assessments project your stock understanding and preserve your mind going for walks in alignment with the present day-day training you're approximately to take.

Quizzes measure the quantity to which you presently understand a topic. You can quiz your self within the middle of analyzing a lesson in order to test how nicely you comprehended the training.

Testing yourself even in advance than information the mission matter permits improve future reading. A 2009 research posted within the Journal of Experimental Psychology positioned out that students who often did pre-exams have a excessive risk of appearing well in a publish-take a look at. This is proper notwithstanding the fact that the pre-take a look at questions were answered incorrectly.

Pre-checks feature early exposure to the crucial element standards and terms on the way to be described in a while inside the schooling. This publicity is proper because the extra you word, pay attention, and consider a certain term in a pre-test, the higher the risk of retaining requirements approximately it in a while.

Quizzing your self as you traverse the education allows you emerge as aware about the concepts you're having a difficult time records. You also can then pinpoint those specific topics and allot greater time to studying them inside the destiny.

Frequently answering workout questions earlier than and all through a lesson makes you higher at check-taking. It hones your trying out talents together with:

? Wrong-solution removal

? Making knowledgeable guesses

? Time-attention at the same time as taking an examination

All those talents are at paintings at the equal time as you are taking a pre-check or quiz and are being honed even in case you get wrong answers at a few stage in the assessments.

Quizzing oneself is a great reading technique in case you are willing to the logical, interpersonal, intrapersonal, and linguistic learning patterns. But you can nevertheless get the blessings noted above even if you have superb tactics to reading.

Incorporating Pre-Tests and Quizzes in Your Study Sessions

Building a addiction of taking tests earlier than and at the same time as you have a look at is a courageous choice. Lots of university college students inclusive of you revel in jitters and tension in the course of assessments. What greater if you're about to take a take a look at with you having nearly zero statistics about the subject to hand?

The reason why college students experience afraid in taking pre-assessments is the perception that they want to despite the fact that get high grades in spite of the reality that they realise little about the take a look at subjects.

But this wondering isn't proper. Pre-assessments are designed to introduce novices to the most important requirements within the instructions. And it's high-quality even if you don't get the right answers, What topics most is that you've got a brief evaluation of the lesson you're approximately to have a look at.

So how do you incorporate pre-exams and quizzes during your observe periods? Here are a few pointers:

? Save the pre-checks that your instructors have given you at college. Skim through them one more time at domestic and be aware about the rationales blanketed within the right answers.

? Obtain copies of ready-made tests and quizzes associated with the training you'll be reading. Make wonderful that there's a solution key and rationales for the best solutions. Use the ones exams as a assessment both in advance than you observe a unit or as you pass along the training.

? Take your pre-tests at domestic as you may within the lecture room. Use test-taking strategies and maintain in thoughts of the time.

? Try to endure in mind the phrases and mind you've seen in your pre-tests. Those are in all likelihood the essential issue facts which you need to recognize about the difficulty depend.

? Take quiz breaks now and again as you check. Several textbooks and reviewers have stop-of-unit quizzes; use them for your benefit.

Tests aren't in reality machine to assist instructors affirm a pupil's getting to know improvement. They can also facilitate getting to know in its private right. This is the truth in the back of the usage of pre-tests earlier than a lesson is studied and quizzes in among reading classes.

Pre-exams and quizzes cover quite a lot the crucial issue ideas you need to have a study in a subject or lesson. Note that the checks are already hinting you at which records you want to attention on. And as you're uncovered to key phrases and mind in a take a look at, you'll get higher comprehension and retention while you do come across them as you've got a take a look at the lesson.

Ready-made quizzes and exams may be used to contain pre-attempting out before analyzing at domestic. These usually come from reviewer books and give up-of-unit questionnaires in textbooks. They are frequently discovered by using rationales maintaining the reason behind accurate answers in the exam.

It takes a chunk of having used to earlier than you can completely add tests on your every day have a study repertoire. But be recommended through the fact that trying out does wonders to your memory, statistics, and retention, regardless of getting the proper answers or no longer.

Chapter 2: Psychological Solutions For Effective Learning

The biggest hassle in recent times is restrained time. You have lots to take a look at but don't have sufficient time. If it's far critical to now not only examine more in tons much much less time but additionally undergo in mind it for an extended duration.

Becoming a person who learns correctly and effectively doesn't display up in just one or weeks, you need to exercise each day a number of those highbrow solutions for effective and green studying.

1.   Learn and Practice New Things Regularly

Regularly studying and running toward new matters permits you turn out to be an powerful and inexperienced learner. It is due to the fact ordinary juggling with new thoughts increases the amount of gray be counted variety in the location of your mind related with visible reminiscence.

For Example

If you are getting to know Digital Marketing, it is critical to frequently exercising/ located into effect some trouble you've located out. It will assist you examine more efficiently.

2.   Teach Another Person

Educators say that sharing newly determined knowledge and abilities with a few different individual is a awesome way to analyze some detail. Doing so solidifies that facts in your mind.

For Example

If you are analyzing a modern day route, find out some character you can train the stuff you've observed. Another great manner is to create a podcast, write a weblog put up, or take part in corporation discussions.

three.   Learn In Different Ways

Another technique to research successfully is to have a look at some element in multiple strategies. As a chunk of information stored in first-rate areas of the thoughts interconnects them. Pulling out facts from a couple of garage place is straightforward.

For Example

If you are getting to know some detail with the beneficial useful resource of following the aural style of reading (permit's say being attentive to an audiotape or podcast), try to rehearse visually and verbally as nicely. Take notes of what you have got were given observed out or describe it to a person else.

four.   Practice Relational Learning

You can take a look at more correctly by using education relational studying. It way bearing on the modern-day information you'll examine with the subjects already appeared to you.

For Example

If you are mastering martial arts, you'll in all likelihood relate it with what you understand about it; wherein it belongs to, your favored movie star who does martial arts, or extremely good facts associated with it.

5.   Don't Struggle, Just Find Answers

Remember, the getting to know technique isn't always best. Sometimes, human beings neglect a few records about some thing already located. Studies say that longer time spent to consider something increases the chances to miss about it over again within the destiny.

For Example

If you found out about a state-of-the-art recreation a few days once more and now you could't do not forget all its instructions, the remarkable you ought to do is look for them without wasting any time. It will limit the probabilities of forgetting it once more inside the future.

6.   Get Practical Experience

Most human beings anticipate that studying includes attending lectures, taking notes, analyzing textbooks, or studying on the internet. For inexperienced gaining knowledge of, you need to placed the acquired records to exercise.

For Example

If you're analyzing Spanish, workout it thru often talking with community Spanish audio device or begin looking movies inside the Spanish language.

7.   Understand Your Learning Style

Another fantastic way to decorate studying is via being aware about your gaining information of favor. According to the concept of Gardner, there are in wellknown eight extremely good types of getting to know (discover them in financial smash 2). By knowledge which one is yours, you may get huge help.

For Example

If you studies effectively with song on foot inside the historic beyond, your gaining knowledge of favor is Aural. As track doesn't distract you, find out which kind of tune lets in you examine in the tremendous way.

eight.   Boost Learning With Testing

A not unusual perception is that making an funding extra time to have a study maximizes gaining knowledge of. A few researchers provide an reason of that checks are what enables you don't forget the data you've found for a long term.

For Example

If you are a college pupil, appear for some mock assessments concerning your path. You can remember matters about your direction better, although they were now not inside the assessments. Compare your recalling functionality to the time in advance than mock tests.

9.   Set Short-Term Goals

By putting short-term goals, you venture your self to do a particular amount of hard work in a confined time. When you observe the concept of reason installing studying, you get the incentive to investigate correctly.

For Example

If you're are a pupil, assignment yourself to finish getting to know 3 chapters in weeks. Track your progress so you recognize whether or not or now not you're going the right manner or no longer.

10. Avoid Multitasking

A commonplace notion is that humans doing multiple responsibilities at a time are superior or above-common. But multitasking influences studying due to the fact at the same time as you switch among particular duties, you'll get bored and lots of time. Multiple responsibilities result in slow and lots less green mastering.

For Example

If you are worried in multiple duties, in conjunction with reading, operating, and playing soccer, you'll waste a whole lot of time going from college to place of job after which to the soccer floor. Also, you may locate it difficult to pay interest.

Chapter 3: Excessive Reversed Repetition

Critical information permits you to nearly study ideas you test from a selected e-book or lecture. It's an extraordinary way of mastering but the reality remains that now not all examination questions are primarily based mostly on critical statistics.

Most college students are nice to come upon questions that focus on the capability to bear in mind and regurgitate textual content ebook data onto the exam paper - Don't mistake this for plagiarism.

I studied regulation, extra particularly, South African Law. This supposed that in an effort to nicely bypass wonderful examinations, I had to proper away don't forget provisions of the Constitution or Bill of Rights and quote onto paper.

There is an smooth generation to recalling particular records and records – it's known as Excessive Repetition. By studying, speakme, writing and hearing the equal piece of data again and again another time, it can get assigned to your memory each short term and long term relying at the frequency and length of time you spend on excessive repetition.

To take it a notch a higher, excessive reversed repetition is a way of repeating content material fabric from the prevent to the start. That way, while running with notes, start from the primary net page and maintain to the last after which begin from the very last web page until you get decrease back to the primary net page. Repeat this for as often as you want.

What I love to do is divide my notes into classes:

Things I Need To Learn By-Heart Over Months

Things I Can Learn By-Heart Over Night

Things I want to investigate via-coronary heart over months are commonly lengthy, drawn out thoughts that span one hundred's of pages. They require a aggregate of realistic and theoretical assessment coupled with periodical study.

These are the sort of sections or subjects that clearly require immoderate repetition over explosive repetition.

Note-making is going an extended way on the subject of massive subjects.

Shorter content material cloth like theoretical based totally sincerely topics which I can summarize in linear notes can without trouble be learnt by means of-coronary coronary heart in a single day. Excessive repetition works quite well for these styles of sections.

They are easy to apprehend, simplified variations made with the aid of the use of you and can be discovered inside a few hours because of the truth regurgitation onto the examination paper is all that's required (forgive me for the usage of the phrase regurgitation, lol).

-] Self-Test & Analysis [-

Y

ou can't recognize what you don't understand. You can exquisite understand what you don't recognize by means of checking out your self.

Wow, that turned into a chunk of a tongue tornado!

No one is nice and now not even the draw close of his very private design is constantly capable of remembering or recalling each unmarried element of his work.

It's not a sign of failure or loss of coaching. Our brains are sponges. It soaks up as plenty facts from the whole thing we are exposed to. Through all that exposure, every, vital and unessential records, are stored in our brains.

Like a sponge, on the identical time because it receives too entire, it starts offevolved to leak and so as for it to soak up extra content material fabric, it desires to permit glide of information. Thus, we forget about about subjects. Especially subjects that we do now not make a conscious effort of remembering or walking toward.

Nevertheless, at the identical time as you're acquainted with a topic, each by using past revel in or via a quick encounter, it's far a smart glide to check your self preceding to studying to gage your level of records and know-how. What this does is it gives you a few problem to evaluate your finished effects with to gage in reality how a terrific deal you've learnt and mastered at the prevent of your research.

On the opportunity aspect of the spectrum, a take a look at preceding to studying can and could difficult you up a chunk. It's a terrific tool for waking a person up from a long and lazy highbrow near eye. I use this method each time I underestimate the severity of a complex state of affairs. Witnessing utter defeat will pressure you to technique a subject with as a exceptional deal seriousness and commitment as feasible.

But, pleasant do that if you aren't vulnerable to quitting. A susceptible thoughts might also moreover use this take a look at as an excuse to bail. In which case, pass the pre-studying take a look at and maintain it for the exam guidance section.

A word of advice: The notable character cheating themselves is the most effective who quits.

He or she is certainly robbing themselves of boom and prosperity. Nothing profitable in lifestyles comes clean. It's generally the hard subjects which generally tend to bring about an abundance of results and rewards. Rather placed in the difficult paintings, struggle if you have to, persevere and fail time and again over again until you be successful. Afterwards, when you have finally succeeded, the culmination of your tough art work can be out of this worldwide. You will experience unstoppable and not some aspect will definitely be succesful to forestall you. Things will virtually try and stop you, they'll even knock you tough sufficient to stumble, however you may get higher even extra tough and knock out any mission that comes your way. This is how a winner is born!

Here's in which subjects get as an alternative interesting. A addiction I've solid over the latter course of my research is to host a mock exam for modules I do now not feel snug with.

I create a ridicule exam timetable and set out cautiously picked dates to imitate my actual timetable. Each mock exam lasts for two hours and in that component, I go to a quiet room, lock myself in, set a timer and write the examination.

About an hour later, I move onto marking my examination paper and isolate the ones arrears which require additional focus.

It without a doubt so takes vicinity that on every occasion I maintain a ridicule exam, the amount of hysteria I face reduces extensively! Exposing your self to uncomfortable situations often will make you revel in extra snug in such conditions as time passes you via the use of manner of.

Consider hosting a mock examination for those modules or subjects that scare you the most.

In time, no exam may be as daunting as they became. Give it a shot and allow me understand the way it seems.

Hey, most importantly, you can song your outcomes. When you acquire that factor of scoring 80% and extra during a ridicule examination, there's be very little to fear while checks appear.

-] The Truth About Examinations [-

E

xaminations are simply used for trying out your records. Most college students have a examine tests as an unwanted length of their life however the actual cause at the back of examination is to evaluate your growth as a scholar.

It is a way of checking out how correctly you could exercise information you studied over the years in sensible take a look at environment. Examinations are not designed to make you fail and neither are there hard or easy examinations. It all is predicated upon on how nicely you understand and prepared for a selected concern count. For someone who spent hour's every day analyzing, making notes, knowledge and repeating vital data is maximum probable high quality to discover an exam simpler than those who don't. In truth, you don't want a herbal knowledge or knack for a topic to be ideal at it – all you require is consistency and hard artwork.

Examinations

No examiner takes pride in failing someone. If anything, they often look for statistics and motives to award you with marks.

You is probably surprised to recognize that a purpose why some humans fail examinations isn't due to the fact they lack records or relevant facts to reply questions but because of the fact their handwriting is ineligible.

An examiner might also have a hard time awarding you crucial marks if he or she cannot make out heads or tails of what you wrote. I used to have horrible handwriting. Combine that with the strain of looking to write rapid sufficient to finish a check inside the allocated time - it looked like worldwide war three broke out on my examination paper.

It's pretty obvious that my untidiness made it pretty tough for examiners and markers to understand coherently what I wrote now not to say look for elements inside my arguments to award me detail marks.

Eventually, I made it a non-public assignment to practice writing through putting aside 10 minutes every day to attempt to cram in as hundreds sentences from a few aspect I study onto a page. I did this with the goal of trying to boom my phrase depend at the same time as assembly a terrific modern of neatness.

Over time, I actually have become capable of enhance my tempo of writing with out compromising readability and neatness. This small improvement improved my likeliness of now not simply passing but getting as fine of a mark in examinations as possible. It's not just the manner you write that subjects, it's the manner you gift facts on paper.

I understand that many textbooks are written as an alternative 'intriguingly' with quite a load of jargon too.

Merely seeking out to attract information from those books and writing pretty complexly without it being a demand for a question makes it hard for markers to gage what you're pronouncing.

It's instead smooth to lose reputation and burst off topic while running underneath stress but so that you can win as many marks as feasible; you need to emerge as aware of as many stable elements as feasible. You can do this thru the usage of replicating a word making form on the equal time as writing.

I won't dive into that right now due to the truth we are capable of get to word making in some. For now, what you need to recall is that the much less complicated you're making it to your examiners to understand your arguments and reasoning for a specific query, the likelier it is that you can get provided the most marks.

Another issue to understand is that examination questions can each be theoretical or practical in nature. Often, they consist of keywords along with the subsequent:

Discuss or Explain – Can be both wide or extensively executed. Such questions are designed to acquire a pinnacle stage view or an extensive evaluation of all the records applicable to the question. You are authorised to combine hundreds of techniques inclusive of listing developments, evaluating arguments, identifying drawbacks and so on.

Identify and Define – Very specific in nature. Requires a scholar to mention concise and nearly proper theories and standards blanketed over the route. Generally, such questions are targeted at thoughts which might be made from ranges or interrelated terms that form part of a way.

Compare – These questions require you to not fine find out unique tendencies of sections however to talk approximately how they variety from every specific and the way each also can create a selected give up end result. You might also moreover issue out the blessings and negatives of every issue and the way they range from every unique.

List Similarities – This is any other identification question that requires you to say developments, virtues and characteristics that healthful 2 one-of-a-kind sections or thoughts making them much like every outstanding. Sometimes, this kind of query calls for a feel of deeper expertise as a way to allow you to appeal to similarities that won't be apparent to a person who lacks vital expertise of a phase.

Give Your Opinion – Depending on the mark allocation, questions based totally mostly on scholar critiques are especially used to examine the scholars capabilities of separation, linking, evaluating and forming hypothesis of a selected phase and explaining why, how and at the same time as he or she is of the opinion a sure stop end result may additionally additionally upward thrust up or why it obtained't. You can also even deliver your opinion on quoted texts that aren't from your prescribed have a observe material so long as you're analysing and giving an top sufficient opinion of its relevancy, applicability and usability.

Argumentative – In brief, you want to fight a case as to why you compromise or disagree with a declaration. Imagine you're in courtroom docket and you are arguing in opposition to opposing endorse! You have to look for loopholes in their argument, declaration, records, and assets that verify your beliefs and offer an cause of ways your argument makes greater experience than the opportunity!

Depending on each of these questions, the form in which your solution is made from will decide whether or not or no longer or no longer or not you've replied the query as it have to be.

Another hassle is time manage at some point of examinations.

Papers/ Test are set out on this type of manner that examiners and moderators are of the belief that a stipulated amount of time is enough to finish a take a look at with right enough marks. Thus, questions are created in a way that make sure trustworthy interest is given to all sections of the take a look at fabric in addition to possibilities as a way to rating essential marks. It is your duty to grow to be aware of in reality how a tremendous deal content material fabric cloth and time is needed in line with question. You can do this with the aid of the use of first identifying the kind of query being asked as I really have indicated with the keywords above and then have a look at the mark allocation. A query for two marks will maximum probably require about 2 – three lines of applicable records and in a few times which includes actual and faux questions, in reality affirming proper or faux can earn you 1 - 2 marks.

An essay question for 20+ marks requires a aggregate of statistics, critiques, comparisons, similarities and arguments. You would possibly manifestly want to dedicate a large quantity of time for an essay question than a 2 mark query. If you have got been to spend 2 mins on a 2 mark query, then multiplying that via manner of 10 for a 20 mark query appears suitable because it's 10 instances greater marks.

The identical components can be used for the quantity of content cloth an essay query might also require. Simply placing ahead 3 lines of textual content isn't going to earn you 20 marks! However, 20 lines also can do the trick! My enjoy with essays appears to deliver me to the perception that examiners are searching out how properly you may take thoughts and concepts and collect an essay in in which the entirety suits collectively in synchrony and creates a large image that covers what is anticipated from the essay difficulty count.

An introduction, body and cease make up the essential shape of an essay.

Closing up, make yourself acquainted with the only of a kind types of questions you may encounter within the exam and are trying to find for out high-quality solutions.

Chapter 4: Universal Advice

Always Know What is Ahead and What is Behind

It's easy to get slowed down in details, specifically in a truth heavy science class like Chemistry. Constant memorization and regurgitation of cloth is tiresome and it's clean to lose sight of the big photograph. I think it's important to stability a massive photo view with the info so that you can see in which each piece you examine suits. This will assist you do nicely in the end. If you recognize how and why the information you're studying is being layered, you could don't forget greater of what you look at. The reason for that could be a idea called chunking.

Chunking is a manner of categorizing facts in levels. For example, if we begin with car, we will chew up to transportation. We may additionally want to then bite proper right down to a completely unique method of transportation, like educate, bus, bicycle, or aircraft. We also can chunk down from automobile to Volvo, Mazda, Ford, or Nissan. The farther you chunk up, the nearer you are to the large photograph. Chunking up is like zooming out. The farther you chunk down, the greater sure the records turns into. You need to maintain chunking down from automobile to engine, piston, oil, all of the manner proper down to molecules in case you preferred. All information is a huge internet of information, a big flowchart–chunking is the manner you navigate the internet. When you're taking a category, you're getting to know the information of some particular place of the net, or how to make use of a specific region. For example, in case you take a writing class you enhance your potential to prepare components of language. If you do not forget gaining knowledge of in phrases of chunking, you'll be able to do not forget extra statistics due to the fact the higher levels will remind you of data in lower degrees.

Ask Questions

Unless you live in a dungeon, chances are you've been given this advice a thousand instances. There is a cause for that: it's brilliant advice. The aspect of college is education. You'll study more in case you ask questions. Ask questions on the whole lot you don't apprehend. If you revel in awkward or uncomfortable talking up in beauty, right here's why I expect you need to rethink. If I don't recognize some component, I need to ensure I recognize some thing, or if I'm simply curious approximately something associated with the material, I ask about it. The teachers are constantly happy I requested the questions, and you will be surprised to recognize that scholars are frequently satisfied too. Hundreds of humans have arise to me after beauty and thanked me for asking questions in elegance due to the fact they were too afraid to ask them. I've made buddies, take a look at companions, even been invited to events right now because of asking a question in class (no humorous story!). If you cannot supply your self to raise your hand, write down your questions and both ask them after beauty, or research them your self. The school room is the region to ask questions.

There is a notable tale that illustrates this element. During World War One, Henry Ford modified into classified with the useful useful resource of a Chicago newspaper as ignorant and pacifistic. He did now not agree, so he sued the newspaper. In the court docket docket, the legal professional for the other aspect positioned Ford on the witness stand and started out out to invite him all kinds of questions, with the purpose to reveal that he end up ignorant. After an extended line of specific questions about information and exceptional subjects, Ford have end up bored with it. He spoke up and stated some issue along the strains of, "I understand don't the exact technique to your question. But on my table, I sincerely have a row of buttons, and with the resource of pushing the proper button I can name a person to reply any question I simply have." Everyone in the courtroom docket recognize how effective of an answer this changed into, that Ford changed into now not an ignorant man. He understood that an sensible individual is aware of the manner to locate the information they want. Asking questions is one of the notable methods to discover the statistics you're looking for.

Create Your Own Study Aids

Not all training is probably advanced with the aid of observe aids, however any class that requires memorization will likely advantage. Whether you want to memorize vocabulary, records, or formula, developing your personal fabric is a top notch concept. The best way to do this is to install writing the whole lot you want to apprehend on a have a observe sheet and take a look at thru it regularly. This has a few weaknesses, especially that the facts is in the equal order whenever. This will create associations among phrases which is probably near every special, making them more difficult to endure in mind outside of the have a have a look at sheet context. Flash gambling playing cards are the subsequent step up. Not first-rate are you able to separate out playing playing playing cards which you have already memorized, you may shuffle them among intervals just so each piece of statistics you research has an unbiased don't forget.

Study aids may have extraordinary programs as well. I created a complete set of printable flash playing cards for a systematic terminology beauty I took, and that they've been so easy and powerful that I determined to promote them to 1-of-a-kind college college students. I ended up offering the gambling playing cards for sale on Amazon, and their achievement introduced approximately me to create specific material to help human beings achieve studying. Had I now not created those flash cards, opportunities are you'll now not be studying this e-book proper now.

Other techniques of memorization can be in particular powerful for associated statistics. Mnemonics, for instance, permit you to don't forget small series of statistics. In track, Every Good Boy Deserve Fudge allows college college students remember the order of notes for sheet track in the treble clef. In Chemistry, OIL RIG permits university students do not forget the motion of electrons for oxidation and cut price. Oxidation Is Loss, Reduction Is Gain. Another famous mnemonic for this is "LEO the lion is going GER." Lose Electrons Oxidation, Gain Electrons Reduction. You can create a mnemonic for something you need to memorize.

Use Your Resources

Know Where to Find the Information You Need

Recall the story approximately Henry Ford. He knew exactly in which to find out the data he wanted. As a end result, no longer handiest did he make a huge fortune, he changed the area. Knowing in which to discover the proper facts is especially crucial if you want to acquire college. Information can be supplied in textbooks, and via way of the use of your instructors, but as a way to get the maximum out of that information you have to use it correctly, and fill in the gaps that amplify. Everyone is privy to records in a great manner, so the gaps that increase might be one-of-a-type for every body. Your teachers are one of the super sources, as are one-of-a-kind college students in your education. Always ask questions when you have them, and are trying to find out the answers to questions your trainer or one-of-a-kind students can not answer. The library and the net are specific first rate assets. You university most probable has programs installation to help you locate the statistics you need: test centers, tutoring, assist desks. Use them!

Determine the Most Important Information inside the Course

What Should You Spend the Most Time Studying?

Every path is designed to educate you a few component. There are commonly center skills you'll be predicted to understand. Mastering the ones capabilities first will now not simplest enhance your grade, but will assist you examine the information that fill inside the picture. In a records elegance, it might be better than you memorize a fundamental chronology of the term you are reading, rather than a slew of dates and names. In technology, understanding the large photo properly will typically assist you fill within the info. You can use the concept of chunking (stated inside the phase "") that will help you keep in mind most of the data. If you memorize the information, but they haven't any context, it'll not best be hard to hold in mind them, however to apply them to some factor else however exactly what you observed out. Science in particular is prepared using knowledge from one detail to each different, building on what you've got positioned out and seeing how it contributes to the large picture. Every problem has its very very very own model of this concept. You need to decide what the most important data is. A suitable manner to do this is to ask the trainer what the essential skills of the path are. Ask them about the big picture. Ask them which standards are the maximum essential inside the path. Spend extra time analyzing those subjects. This is not to suggest which you forget about about the facts. Details ought to be placed inside the context of the big photograph.

Feed Your Brain What it Needs to Think

Your thoughts is a complex system. It needs the right gasoline to art work properly. Eating wholesome will improve your grades, because of the reality your thoughts will artwork higher. You will maintain in mind greater, think quicker, and recognize new thoughts greater brief. A diet plan isn't always within the scope of this e-book, but proper right here are a few recommendations to get you started out.

Eat a weight loss plan immoderate in appropriate fat. Eat coconut oil, avocados, fish. Take omega-three supplements. Eat surrender end result and greens. Take a multivitamin that has big quantities of everything you brain desires to feature. Avoid sugar. Avoid capsules and alcohol– they simply do reason your brain to not to art work as properly. I furthermore endorse getting an high-quality quantity of physical interest, cardiovascular exercises are top notch. While we're on the fitness hassle, I additionally endorse you look at an top notch, healthy sleep time table. I am a persistent insomniac, so I continuously stress the significance of having sufficient accurate sleep. If you're worn-out, the chemical materials on your mind that permit it to feature might be unbalanced. These neurochemical imbalances will make it tough to expect proper away, take into account information, anticipate significantly, treatment troubles, make longterm memories, and lots of various subjects that you do not want. Hydration is likewise very important. Drink lots of water.

Chapter 5: How to Manage your Time

Time manipulate is critical in growing effective have a look at behavior. Without proper time management, it's smooth to experience crushed through manner of the endless duties handy. If you want to acquire achievement, you want to discover ways to make the most of some time. This entails organizing and prioritizing your unique school activities and responsibilities so you'll constantly have time on your fingers. If you constantly discover yourself walking out of time, right here are 5 time manage strategies that will help you have a look at more successfully. Ch0ose one that could nice in shape your studying fashion.

Block off examine time

As quick as you get your class time table, set and boom your study time blocks. Ideally, every observe block want to be approximately 50 minutes. According to specialists, that is the longest time your mind can be capable of reputation on a particular venture efficaciously. After the 50 minutes of excessive look at, use the 10 minutes to lighten up and put together art work for the subsequent have a look at block. Since a block off gadget permits the thoughts get used to regular, this is the correct technique for college college college students who do higher following schedules.

Compartmentalize study time

On the alternative hand, if you're the kind who can't stand analyzing for an hour immediately, you could strive compartmentalizing your test time. This is proper for people who should as a substitute take a look at in 10, 20, or 30 minute commands in among unique responsibilities. If you've got the tendency to lose interest with out difficulty, then you truly should probable find it more inexperienced reading in shorter but extra not unusual increments in the route of the day. Setshort have a take a look at lessons on every occasion you may and preserve a timer available so that you'll recognize whilst to prevent.

Familiarize over multiple commands

Having a hard time studying a topic at one flow? Then use the familiarization technique to preserve vital facts. Don't try to memorize a whole bankruptcy in a single sitting. Space it out and do it over a couple of periods. By going via the monetary catastrophe a couple of instances, it's your long time reminiscence so that it will take maintain near of the statistics, not the quick time period one. So in place of spending 60 mins searching for to memorize a financial catastrophe, spoil it down into 3 elements. 25 minutes within the morning studying the primary half of the bankruptcy every other 25 minutes within the afternoon to look at the second half of and 10 minutes earlier than going to bed to skim through the entire monetary catastrophe.

Study everywhere

Don'tconstrain yourself to the concept that you can only test at a exquisite location. If you're more conducive to analyzing specially locations, then take the possibility to accomplish that. Whether it's on a bench looking in advance to the bus, or in among schooling and events, you may get a few analyzing done in quick portions of time. Luckily these days, you don't want to lug spherical heavy books to get get proper of entry to to statistics. You can hold notes or text to your Smartphone or iPad, or in case you're extra traditional, you could preserve photocopies of key pages from lectures folded on your notes. This lets in you to make the most out of idle time you may commonly be spending doing not some thing.

Zone in on your pinnacle hours

Experts be given as actual with that our ability to memorize records peaksat first rate instances. So it's a matter of information your self nicely sufficient to discover whether you're a morning person, or an midnight man or woman.

If you awaken within the morning s with a clean mind, then your handiest time for reviewing is as soon as you wake up. On the opposite hand, in case you revel in extra conscious throughout nights, you then definately must compare your notes in advance than going to sleep. Different human beings have one in every of a kind top hours so it's truly pretty lots placing your review time at the same time as your thoughts is the maximum active.

Learning the way to control time will permit to you accomplish extra responsibilities with a lot less try. By handling a while well, you'll be to your manner to growing observe conduct for lifestyles.

Chapter 6: Decoding Your Study

The key to studying any scenario efficaciously is your take a look at method!

But, severa university university college students make the error of using the equal observe method for each trouble.

Pre-making plans and Analysis:

Analyzing and making plans your observe this may be your first step.

So, earlier than you begin your have a study, you've got got to research your subjects and subjects.

By information what to have a have a look at and what kind of to test allows you in devising your check plans and additionally, allows you discover which smart take a look at strategies to apply.

For example,

If you have got end up prepared for a test, there may be no point to test 'cowl to cowl' of your textbook.

Studying simply what's required with the aid of way of the syllabus might be enough.

Don't spend an excessive amount of time reading specific miscellaneous facts given inside the textbook.

If your reason is to actually have a have a look at for the exam:

Find out what type of questions may be asked within the examination. Then divide your topics counting on their precedence and weightage as consistent with the examination element.

Try taking the assist of the previous twelve months's questions papers to get an concept. Once you understand your prevent reason. You can plan out the time and electricity you need to invest inside the challenge.

Gather your study materials and constantly try to investigate from the high-quality supply! Take the help of your teachers and buddies while in need.

Know that each difficulty is particular.

Therefore every of them calls for a particular have a have a look at technique to take a look at THAT difficulty higher.

You can not use the identical Smart Techniques which you use to have a examine every statistics and technology! These are specific topics therefore, their observe technique and methods can be unique.

It is viable, from time to time you can want to apply greater than 1 smart approach for a particular mission counting on the topics within the problem.

Key Points:

I'm reading math! Math isn't to be study! It wishes to be practiced!

The have a look at approach you operate for maths can't be used to have a observe records. And the Strategy used for records can't be used for era.

Take to time to attempt to apprehend which smart take a look at techniques given in this ebook can be used.

Technique #1

#1 - Self Quizzing

This is an powerful test method that lets you recall and recall the ideas better.

It moreover lets you store time.

The golden rule of this approach is you observe a topic.

Then you're taking a quick pause sometimes to ask your self a few idea-scary questions without looking on the textual content.

While you ask yourself the questions, you furthermore may additionally additionally try and write down your solutions.

This lets you deal with the center concept of the topic.

When you pick out out a bankruptcy or a subject, try dividing it into chunks. Which is dividing it right into a paragraph or an internet web page.

Next what you do is - have a look at it more than one times.

Now without looking at the textual content, reflect onconsideration on the types of questions you could ask on a quiz or take a look at. Such as -

'What is the critical aspect context of the financial break/paragraph?'

'What are the critical key factors?'

'What is new to you?'

'What did you apprehend?'

Write down your answers.

Make certain to verify your solution ultimately.

Writing the answers for your very own, make you extra confident. By verifying your answers, you can grow to be privy to the strength and weaknesses of the difficulty.

This take a look at method comes very handily when you have a massive aspect to take a look at. By dividing the topics into small chucks you keep away from the strain of take a look at.

Quizzing is an antidote for forgetfulness. Forgetting is human nature. By no longer checking out your self - you overestimate your capacity. Quizzing yourself while you have a look at facilitates you choose out your regions of energy and weakness inside the difficulty depend.

It moreover offers you a pinnacle degree view of techniques a whole lot you without a doubt apprehend and what form of you want to observe.

You can down load the ones unfilled template right here

Technique #2

Isn't it traumatic at the same time as you forget about what you have studied?

When you are all prepared for an exam after which at the same time as you in the long run hit the revision, you realise that you have forgotten maximum of your examine.

So, you turn out to be reading it again.

Many university college students regardless of analyzing well are not capable of remember what they have got studied within the path of the tests. They emerge as getting burdened among thoughts and begin to doubt the entirety.

So, Why can't we keep in mind them?

Our reminiscences may be complex. We may be capable of consider some random statistics have a look at years ago and but proper now forget what we've just have a look at minutes in the past.

It's due to the truth our reminiscences are labeled into brief time period and long time reminiscences. Whenever a modern-day day piece of records is obtained they're saved into quick time period reminiscence.

Short term recollections get faded with time. Unless they may be recalled every so often.

When quick time period reminiscences are recalled they then grow to be a long term reminiscence. These reminiscences then are retained for a longer time.

Whenever a bit of records is obtained via our senses (eyes and ears) - If this information is not paid interest they'll be out of location (no active learning).

But if given attention to, they will be saved into brief term memory (i.E in case of active mastering), but those memories are saved pleasant for a short time. Hence the recollections fade away.

In case the equal reminiscence is retrieved from time to time. If it's far recalled again and again.

This reminiscence gets transferred into long time memory and the facts is saved for an extended time.

Think of your mind as a laptop. When you placed a file proper right into a laptop it receives processed and stored. But this laptop has a very unique way to perform.

It slowly erases fragments of information if that information isn't used. In case in case you on occasion test those statistics, it recognizes as essential and eventually keeps it.

This is similar to the way our memories artwork.

To maintain the records that we've got studied ought to be recalled occasionally and time and again.

Here we use the Spaced Repetition Technique. This is the maximum powerful technique for improving your mind's capability to recollect. This method helps you to convert brief term reminiscence into long term reminiscence.

Technique #2

Spaced repetition:

Spaced repetition is all approximately introducing time periods amongst check classes. In essence, we look at extra than as speedy as however through way of way of leaving considerable time amongst have a observe periods.

We do this with the resource of scheduling a revision.

So essentially at the same time as you're completed studying a subject. Next, you suggest out it gradual periods for the revisions.

For instance; you may take a look at a subject nowadays. You can time desk your 1st revision after 2 days.

Then the 2nd revision after four days from the first revision.

1/3 after eight days from second revision and so on.

This manner you may red meat up your memory and improve your functionality to hold in mind.

"Exercise in time and again recalling a problem strengthens the reminiscence" Aristotle.

You ought to unfold out some time periods. If you do now not go away sufficient time between your revision. It will be simply some other rote gaining knowledge of so location out your take a look at to avoid mindless repetition.

This is the most effective reminiscence approach. This no longer simplest allows you preserve your ideas longer to your memory. But additionally help you recall them genuinely.

How to use this technique;

Step 1 - Study a topic.

Step 2 - Schedule your revision.

Step 3 - Quiz your self after every scheduled revision.

Step 4 - Brush up the topics which you do not hold in mind well.

You may additionally moreover need to apply your phone calendar reminders to remind you of your revision time table. Also, ensure to assess your quiz solutions through using scoring your self. You can use quiz questions from the preceding technique.

You can down load these unfilled template proper proper here

Technique #3

The Random Problem Method

Mixing things up!

In this method, you have a look at multiple kind of problem interior a subject at a time.

Example; While analyzing physics formulas or maths have a have a look at multiple kind of trouble at a time. This way you're alternating amongst precise forms of troubles that require brilliant answers.

Quizzing your self on numerous problem kinds, facilitates your mind to differentiate amongst ideas greater thoroughly. Strengthens your memory affiliation.

By blending topics up will make you continuously undertaking your capability to recognize the trouble kind and pick out out the proper answer.

Consider a cricket batsman- who practices batting thru swinging at 20 fastballs, then 20 slower balls, and then 20 spin balls. This shape of participant will perform better in exercising than the player who mixes it up.

However, the participant who mixes things up via the use of swinging at wonderful pitches at some point of schooling builds his capability to decipher and reply to each ball because it comes his manner at some point of the suits, thereby turning into a higher batsman.

The give up end result of the Random Problem Method improves your achievement in later assessments in that you want to differentiate the kind of hassle you're searching for to solve to use the appropriate solution.

While you can enjoy this sort of approach is unproductive/ counterproductive or cause confusion between standards. But, the alternative is real.

Studying more than one detail is to be endorsed to beautify your reading capability.

So within the route of checks, you don't get forced approximately which technique to apply at the same time as comparable problems are asked.

Mixing troubles no longer only assist you determine out the way to do a trouble however moreover which techniques to use.

For instance, in math. The critical capacity to resolve a trouble is to use the proper method to remedy the proper trouble. Many university students perform poorly in math due to this cause. Because they get forced about comparable problems and attempt to use a method that isn't supposed for that trouble.

This method enables you emerge as privy to that. Interleaving permits you growth that capacity.

Instead of fixing 10 multiplication troubles, then 10 department problems than 10 additions. Mixing them up lets in you select out the similarities and variations among the trouble sorts.

It allows you assessment older mind and broaden the capabilities needed to pick the right method for solving troubles.

How to apply:

Pick a topic, as an example, say a math hassle. Identify what number of types of troubles or formula are there.

Next, you need to understand what makes them unique and the manner.

What steps are similar

Interchange the troubles or components and remedy them.

Review your solutions.

Technique #4

SQ3R technique

These days take a look at substances are given in numerous formats.

Some are films, audios, and most of the look at substances are in written layout.

Sometimes you've got got pages of records to have a look at. It gets tougher to examine all of it. Understanding the cloth and staying focused receives more and more tough if you don't apprehend a way to optimize what you look at.

This technique simplifies your reading time and helps you to have a observe, understand, consider written data greater quick.

SQ3R stands for -

Survey,

Question,

Read,

Recite, and

Review.

Step #S- Survey;

The first step:

You take a minute to go through the subject.

You try to be aware about the shape of the hassle which include format, most crucial factors, heading, sub-heading, or different subtopics together with figures, tables, marginal records, and precis.

In desired, you try and recognize the primary context of the given topic with the aid of way of the usage of NOT studying the whole thing!

This usually takes some minutes.

Step #Q- Questions

Once you're accomplished scanning.

Ask your self questions about the problem.

Think of yourself as an examiner who is making an attempt to make up a question paper. For instance, try converting headings and subheadings into questions.

Next, you ask yourself more trendy questions on the side of,

What is that this economic catastrophe about?

How does this data help me?

What is this bankruptcy looking for to teach?

What did I realise already?

Draw a vertical line on the paper, write your questions about the left and later you can answer them at the right.

Step #R1 - Read

When you're finished making up the questions. Next step, you begin to examine actively.

When you look at you try to pay close to hobby to chapters, headings, and reasons. This step, You read the challenge in extra detail in area of absolutely skimming.

When required you may write down greater questions as you look at. While you furthermore mght try to answer the preceding questions.

Take it slow to look at greater complicated subjects.

The difference among passive and lively have a observe is that during passive reading is you slightly study with out engaging deep into the difficulty. Active studying is you pay hobby and have interaction deep into the topic.

Step #R2 - Retrieve

This step is all approximately the manner you retrieve the information located out from your reminiscence using your non-public terms. You try and make a summary of the concept found out.

You can do this every orally or written whichever you revel in cushty. One of the tremendous techniques to recall and make sure you understand the concern is to give an cause of it to someone in a smooth way feasible.

Think of yourself as a trainer who is making an attempt to teach a child.

Albert Einstein said, "If you can't offer an explanation for it truly, you do no longer recognize it nicely enough."

Albert Einstein used to provide an purpose in the back of his complicated principle of relativity as, "When a person sits with a quite woman for an hour, it looks as if a minute. But allow him take a seat on a heat stove for a minute—and it's miles longer than an hour. That's relativity."

Step #R3 - Review

This is probably the final step. Once you achieve the prevent of the subject,

Read all of the applicable elements another time.

Go via your solutions and confirm them.

You are reviewing the fabric through repeating lower lower back to yourself what you've got take a look at the use of your very personal terms.

SQ3R - Survey permits you put together for check, therefore, efficiently priming your thoughts.

You can down load this unfilled Template right here

Technique #5

So far you have got were given found out the way to take a look at the challenge with out rote mastering, however there are fantastic information that require memorization.

Facts which embody names of planets, Spectrum of colours, Orders of mathematical operations, Trigonometric ratios. Sometimes the ones are without difficulty memorized, sometimes they will be now not and the problem with smooth memorization is that it is with out problem forgotten.

Also in phrases of even more complex facts to bear in mind at the side of names of bones in a human cranium, it becomes difficult to remember them.

One manner to examine ANY reality is to use Mnemonic devices.

Mnemonic gadgets

So, what are Mnemonic Devices?

Mnemonic Devices are Memory cues that assist us preserve in thoughts certain facts or big quantities of information effects.

They can be made up right right into a track, or a rhyme.

They are most normally crafted from an acronym or a word and moreover a sentence.

Mnemonics help us bear in mind information and are specially useful at the equal time as the order of factors is critical.

Imagine them being like your intellectual report cabinet. A vicinity in which you save the facts and you can retrieve them with out troubles each time you want them.

Let's check out some of the examples on the way to can use a Mnemonic.

To don't forget the names of planets in order:

Mercury, Venus, Earth, Mars, Jupiter, Saturn, Uranus, Neptune, and Pluto.

For this, I can sincerely recollect,

My Very Educated Mother Served Us Nine Pizzas

Do you study the number one letters of the phrases in the given sentence?

M - Mercury

V - Venus

E - Earth

M - Mars

J - Jupiter

S - Saturn

U - Uranus

N - Neptune

P - Pluto

Now if you don't want to include pluto, you may maintain in mind:

My Very Educated Mother Served Us Nacho's

More complicated records which consist of naming the bones in a human cranium.

There are 6 bones in a cranium:

Ethmoid, Temporal, Parietal, Occipital and frontal.

If you want to do not forget them from back to front.

Old People From Taxes Eat Spiders

The use of mnemonic gadgets improves studying normal performance. They help you consider quicker, higher and help you maintain them longer.

More Example:

Memorizing the Electromagnetic Spectrum so as of developing frequency, you can use this acronym/sentence:

Raging Martians Invaded Venus Using X-ray Guns.

The order of increasing frequency of the electromagnetic spectrum is:

Radio,

Microwave,

Infrared,

Visible,

Ultraviolet,

X-rays, and

Gamma rays.

Motive to Study

The fantastic manner to get better at any situation is to method it with a pleasing mind-set. You can't assume to grow a watermelon if you have planted seeds of cucumber. In the identical manner, you can't count on a satisfactory give up result with a horrible thoughts-set. You can't don't forget failing if you need to be successful.

If you need to have a have a look at a topic technique it with a top notch mindset, don't suppose how difficult or how silly that trouble it.

If you do suppose that manner, it is going to be tough and dull for you.

Don't take the opinion of your others as a right.

If they are pronouncing, this problem is tough. Don't ever count on it will likely be the equal for you, attempt it out. Never make up your mind approximately the problem in advance than attempting. Maybe what others find out hard, you could find out it easy.

Never Limit Yourself:

It's very often that students underestimate their abilities. Students with plenty of potentials, who are able to high-quality subjects, restriction themselves now not with the beneficial aid of others however by the usage of their private ideals.

"I can't do this."

"This is an excessive amount of for me. "

"I am no longer that clever. "

It's regularly not their inabilities that save you people from wearing out their goals it's their Beliefs!

They have a predefined notion that they may no longer advantage some thing beyond that point!

So they in no way purpose higher or possibly try to beautify.

To stay inspired, motive a hint better than yesterday. Try to do little more than the day before today. You don't ought to do the whole lot right now. Whatever you do without a doubt do 1% better than yesterday. Each and absolutely everyone is capable of exquisite things simplest if they will recollect and artwork for it.

Have an affirmed notion that you can test any hassle if you wish to.

Always purpose for the Moon, If you pass over you could hit the Star.

Chapter 7: Reading Hacks

Reading is by using manner of an extended manner one of the most tedious duties in essentially any sort of college. The appropriate facts, but, is that most humans go approximately analyzing in a completely inefficient manner. Here's a mystery: reading each single phrase of each unmarried e-book isn't always the extremely good manner to deal with reading! This financial wreck is all about methods you could use to drastically reduce down at the time you spend studying.

Hack #eight

Read the material in advance than the lecture, now not after

This is one of the easiest, extremely good things you could do to drastically beautify your effectiveness as a student. In truth, it's so clean, I'm often baffled how many college college students don't do it.

IN A NUTSHELL: Don't visit any lecture without reading the material you're going to be assigned in advance. That way, the lecture isn't an introduction to the cloth; it's your first revision.

Time requirement: 20-half-hour, but it's far based upon at the venture.

Why? This is a comprehension trouble, typically. If you cross proper right into a lecture in reality unprepared, having in no way heard something approximately the fabric earlier than, it's going to be a good deal more tough to recognize. Even worse, you may be fumbling thru notes, looking for passages in a e-book, which means you're no longer listening to the lecture.

If you look at the cloth you're going to be assigned, you'll have already got a primary understanding of it in advance than you even set foot in the look at room. So, rather than trying to juggle a group of stuff proper now, you may actually pay attention. Even extra importantly, you'll probably have some really high-quality questions that weren't responded at the same time as you have got were given been reading.

And it best makes enjoy, right? Who do you believe you studied might have a better know-how: the scholar who has have a look at the cloth and actively engages in conversation with the professor approximately what he's observe, or the scholar who's simplest half of-listening and seeking to capture up inside the e-book. No brainer!

How? This is going to be simplest with training that provide you with a syllabus, considering maximum syllabi define the studying and homework for every elegance length. Your motive isn't to take a look at the entirety. You don't need to be exquisite some distance earlier. You definitely want be one studying task in advance.

Suppose you're going to elegance on Tuesday, and you already know through the use of looking at the syllabus which you're going to ought to have a observe Chapter eight for subsequent Thursday. Read that bankruptcy in advance than the Tuesday elegance.

Additionally, I determined it's exceptional to do that the night time time in advance than a category. Reading with out a stress (you don't must have a have a look at it; you're definitely getting in advance) can definitely be quite amusing. Plus, studying the material and then sound asleep on it will help you preserve it.

Shortcut: Even if you don't need to (or don't have the time to) examine the financial disaster ahead, you have to truely skim it. We've indexed a few honestly amazing skimming techniques for the duration of this ebook, in order that's a superb region to start. Just, as normally, be careful with skimming; if you're not cautious, you could come to be asking an apparent question. If you're going to skim, do it in fact properly.

Bonus! As a bonus, discover a few other material at the task that isn't analyzing. This is one among our favorite techniques, too, and with accurate cause. Giving yourself a few form of extra medium to tool the facts can considerably boom your expertise. So, even as you examine or skim that bankruptcy, discover yourself a YouTube video or a forum discussion to have a look at. All of this generally takes 20-half-hour, and also you'll be bowled over at how a long way earlier of your classmates you're.

Hack #nine

Learn the artwork of skimming

You don't ought to test the whole lot. Yes, you heard that proper. You don't ought to study everything, and you're not slacking if you don't look at the entirety. The idea that you need to examine each phrase of each ebook you're assigned is a complete delusion, and, for my part, absolutely at odds with how the real global works.

But how do you no longer look at the whole thing and even though contribute to discussions, write specific papers, and whole assignments? Well, grasshopper, you do this with the resource of using getting to know the dark artwork of skimming.

IN A NUTSHELL: Instead of analyzing every word of the assignment, study the primary and very last sentences of every paragraph. As you flow, select out one or two crucial sections and look at those in detail, making pinnacle notes.

Why? This is a time control thing. Sometimes, the exquisite way to have a take a look at is to do subjects except reading. Sometimes, the pleasant way to have a look at is to install writing, or assume, or solve a trouble. You can't do that if you've had been given your nose in a e-book.

Now, in advance than I go with the flow on, I want to make clean because of the fact I simply, definitely don't need you to misconceive this. Reading the cloth is crucial, and also you're going to ought to do it. For a few assignments, you acquired't be capable of simply skim, in particular with, say, a computer technology elegance.

However, for masses of training, you can be genuinely as inexperienced skimming as you will studying each word. In truth, often, you can be greater productive.

In the give up, although, skimming permits you to appreciably lessen down at the time you spend studying without sacrificing the learning, that could unfastened up greater time for a few element mode of analyzing you find out efficient (or, heaven forbid, putting out along with your pals and taking thing in yourself).

How? The idea proper here is not to take a look at now not some thing. Rather, it's to reduce the amount of belongings you want to study by means of the use of approximately half of of and however select out up about 90 five% of the assets you want to apprehend. Here's how you do it.

Read the introduction and the conclusion of some thing it is you're supposed to have a have a look at, and take a look at them first. Reading every the introduction and the realization first will provide you with a pretty suitable concept of what the piece is ready widespread, in order you skim, you'll be capable of choose out out what's important.

Then, take a look at the primary and very last sentence of each paragraph. If you find a section this is in particular crucial, especially hard, or especially interesting, have a look at that phase cautiously, make some notes, and write down some follow up questions.

After you end studying, take 2-three minutes to write down down your mind on what you in reality observe and the way it relates to the whole lot else you've determined in that elegance up to now. This will assist you keep all of the stuff you in reality located.

Shortcut: You can now and again escape with reading just the number one sentence of every paragraph. However, you probable gained't understand the cloth as nicely. For some schooling that's ok (e.G. A category wherein the analyzing is supplemental). For a few, notwithstanding the reality that, that can definitely damage you. So virtually be careful about it.

Research Hacks

Researching is all over again sink for hundreds of human beings. Like with reading, notwithstanding the truth that, it often takes numerous time due to the truth (1) it's not fun, and (2) most humans do it very inefficiently. This financial catastrophe is ready enhancing your studies skills, so you can research approximately instances as fast as your classmates and feature plenty greater amusing doing it!

Hack #10

Supplement your analyzing with a laugh stuff

Hands down, one of the great things about being a scholar nowadays is that you have get proper of entry to to the unmarried only learning tool ever created thru guy: the internet! And which means that it generally doesn't count range what you're getting to know about: you may generally locate some component about it on the net, and some of the time, it's going to be masses extra amusing than pouring over academic texts.

IN A NUTHSELL: Find some distinctive supplemental material (e.G. A YouTube video, discussion board dialogue) this is fun for you, and use it to benefit a better information of anything you're learning approximately.

Why? Listen, we've been actual with each distinctive, proper? So allow's be instantly. Sometimes, some of the belongings you take a look at in a category is absolutely... uninteresting. However, from time to time, it's now not the material itself that's stupid; it is probably the textbook, or the professor, or the component you're analyzing.

Almost all the time, something you're studying about is obtainable on the internet, and there are cool, clever, funny people speakme about it. Or making documentaries approximately it. Or making a song approximately it.

Often, you may have a look at masses greater and feature loads extra fun in case you use those substances to benefit a higher knowledge of the difficulty.

For example, I took a amazing, notable stupid French statistics magnificence my freshman twelve months of college. Everything approximately it have become silly, proper proper right right down to the vintage textbook we had been using. However, there are masses and masses of documentaries at the net approximately French history. When I started out out looking these, I discovered I without a doubt sincerely preferred it. Not simplest was I learning plenty greater than I may also have if I'd truly pressured myself to study a group of boring books, however I decided that those same stupid books had been masses more exciting after searching some simply top notch documentaries.

How? You probably recognize wherein to find out stuff at the internet through way of now, but I'll percentage some of my desired subjects except. The trick right here is the find out the component this is most amusing for you. Personally, I love movies. I additionally love speakme to certainly one of a type people. So, once I have become seeking out some fun, supplemental cloth, I'd watch YouTube documentaries and find out a few exciting Reddit threads.

However, there are loads of brilliant resources to be had. Here are only a few.

YouTube documentaries

Reddit discussions

Free on line lecture rooms like Khan Academy or Academic Earth

Emailing/skyping an expert (you'd be surprised how many are happy to talk with you)

Wikipedia (no, it's no longer evil; extra on this in a 2nd)

Blogs

Shortcut: There's no shortcut! That's sort of the beauty of this tip: it's actually nonobligatory. But making mastering greater fun is top to gaining a absolutely deep information of any situation. With the internet, you could genuinely try this for your self. Pretty incredible, right?

Hack #eleven

Use Wikipedia

One of the subjects that aggravated me maximum in college turn out to be the thoughts-set in the path of Wikipedia. You'll pay attention it in pretty a whole lot each splendor you're in: "Do no longer use Wikipedia as a supply." Well, I wholeheartedly disagree; and, in fact, I expect Wikipedia is one of the unmarried greatest examine equipment ever made.

IN A NUTSHELL: Use Wikipedia to (1) get a number one, large information of your situation and (2) discover exceptional notable property you may take a look at from.

Why? Before we solution the query "Why use Wikipedia?" I anticipate we first have the solution the query "Why is Wikipedia not evil?"

I'd be given as true with that any of the professors who condemn Wikipedia may be great with you the use of an encyclopedia, proper? In my view, any discovered encyclopedia is not almost as unique of a beneficial aid as a continuously updated, continuously edited on-line encyclopedia that could gather statistics in actual time.

The drawback, of course, is that everyone can edit it, it certainly is why people are terrified of it. However, over the years, Wikipedia has established remarkably green at keeping its intellectual integrity. In truth, its editors are almost notorious for ruthlessly reducing wrong or unimportant content material cloth.

In quick, Wikipedia will nearly continuously be greater whole and up to date than most encyclopedias, making it as a minimum a legitimate supply, if now not one of the high-quality possible assets.

So use it! Even if your professors can help you recognise not to, use it. You don't need to cite it. You don't must use it as a source. But use it to complement your reading, find out assets in 1/2 the time, and take part in an excellent dialogue. All of as a way to significantly help you take a look at any trouble.

How? Using Wikipedia is quite easy. First, discover the maximum associated web page to some thing it's far you're studying, and study it. This won't take more than 10 minutes, and it'll provide you with a completely, outstanding modern day information.

Then, use that web page to discover one-of-a-kind related Wikipedia pages, and, if it makes enjoy, examine the ones, too. For instance, in case you're gaining knowledge of approximately dogs, you could look at a few internal hyperlinks to pages on specific breeds or the information of dog domestication... something; you get the idea.

Finally, scroll right all of the manner right down to the all-essential resources segment and spot what you can locate. Pick out and bookmark sources that meet the necessities for a citable supply, so that you can use them in destiny papers (or, in case you're writing a paper, use this segment to discover your first source—or possibly even all of them).

Shortcut: I doubt you'll ever be so pressed for time that you could't have a look at a Wikipedia net web page, however in case you are, you can skim the ones similar to you could some component else (remember our section on the artwork of skimming?). In fact, Wikipedia pages are usually an awful lot less difficult to skim due to the fact they're so well set up.

Bonus! Wikipedia's not the first-class on line encyclopedia. Did you recognise that the Encyclopedia Britannica is likewise on-line? It is. You can also strive Reference.Com and Encyclopedia.Com, if you're inside the temper for some greater browsing.

Chapter 8: Super Foods

Technology has surely modified the location and the whole thing in it. Transportation, communication, manufacturing, and entertainment; the ones are without a doubt few of the matters that technological know-how and research have superior thru the course of humankind. But with all the hype about new gadgets and era, there can be one very vital little bit of era that human beings regularly neglect; food.

Food technology is the area virtually dedicated to accomplished generation regarding food and vitamins. Food is genuinely one of the very simple, however relatively vital, human wishes. The want for food is the primary trait of all residing topics. With the evolution of human way of life, way of existence, and the customers themselves, there can be little emphasis on how high-quality food have an effect on someone's cognitive abilities.

In meals technological know-how, there may be a branch referred to as food generation, which offers particularly with meals manufacturing and techniques. For instance, meals protection (especially Nicolas Appert's canning way in 1810) have become one of the first achievements of meals generation. Of direction, the right intention turned into to increase the shelf-lifestyles of components internal airtight containers.

From then on, meals era became complicated and sundry. Today, humans are now aware about the bad results of a few food techniques in their fitness, in particular fatty and preserved ingredients.

Brain Food Facts

Today's society will pay greater interest to the bad effects of fine components in someone's cardiovascular fitness. This includes health-conscious people who especially worried approximately their weight. Modern meals era once in a while makes use of risky chemical substances in food that could motive coronary heart sicknesses, diabetes, weight issues, most cancers, or maybe thoughts harm.

Unhealthy meals belongings together with rapid food chains and processed substances are created to complement a mean character's fast paced contemporary manner of existence. Most of the time, busy human beings which include professionals and university college college students inn to the ones risky food belongings irrespective of being privy to their bad dietary charge.

Today, a growing extensive kind of consumers begin listening to the link between meals and the mind features.

Numerous studies and research have furnished sufficient proof that what a person eats may have an impact in his intellectual capabilities. These effects can turn out to be awesome both for the long term or brief term.

Foods to Avoid

To start, you could first should make a number of corrections in your modern-day weight loss plan. Unless you were already fitness-conscious as regards to your weight loss program prior to studying this e-book, possibilities are you have been exposed into ingesting them often.

Remember which you do no longer usually want to absolutely dispose of these from your healthy dietweight-reduction plan, however you need to limit them for as a amazing deal as you can.

Fatty Foods – A lot of health ailments these days had been related to the consumption of too much fatty food. Despite being aware of the health risks, plenty of humans although patronize fatty food, this is one of the primary motives for the developing full-size fashion of weight troubles instances in the worldwide. Scientific evidence moreover shows that the consumption of fatty elements can possibly purpose mind harm in some humans.

One study indicates the threat of mind shrinkage for a few folks who eat an excessive amount of fatty components.

Too an awful lot fatty food supply way for some of cognitive complications along with Alzheimer's ailment.

Fatty components impair the hypothalamus area of the thoughts in animal topics. This unique region of the mind is accountable for a number of cognitive features together with moods, dozing cycle, and hunger.

Salty Foods – Evidence indicates that ingesting food with immoderate sodium content material fabric cloth for extended durations motive headaches in a person's coronary heart and thoughts. In a study concerning 1, hundred human individuals, those with a excessive every day intake of sodium were given decrease consequences in cognitive checks than people who had managed intake. Studies additionally show that an excessive amount of consumption of salty food, in particular table salt, can purpose immoderate blood strain, stroke, diverse cardiovascular ailments, and bone illnesses. Remember that sodium is certainly an crucial element of the human frame. An common healthy character want to have a every day sodium consumption of one,500 mg to two,4 hundred mg.

Processed Foods – Foodstuffs are regularly combined with severa chemical materials for precise purposes. These chemical materials or food additives embody preservatives, synthetic food colouring, fructose, artificial flavours, and masses of more. Processed food are tested to have horrible effects in the cognitive functions and development of youngsters. Certain food components which consist of benzoate can also motive hyperactivity. But the maximum volatile chemical that can be positioned in processed meals is Monosodium Glutamate or MSG. This meals additive can kill nerve cells located within the mind. It is probably lethal mainly in specifically immoderate consumptions. Studies furthermore show that one-of-a-type additives can stunt the improvement of the number one concerned system of greater younger youngsters.

Pesticide Residue – Pesticides themselves are existence-threatening for people. Even the smallest trace of the chemical materials in insecticides on positive materials can be volatile for customers. Prolonged publicity to insecticides motives neurological sicknesses like Parkinson's disease. Vegetables and end result from the grocery save are problem to pesticide residue. There are also times of pesticide food poisoning with signs and signs which includes complications, fatigue, susceptible factor, perspiration, nausea, diarrhoea, pores and skin irritation, eye irritation, fever, convulsions, and unconsciousness.

Sometimes the consumption of bad ingredients can not be without a doubt avoided, in particular for humans with worrying schedules who can not plan and put together healthy food at home.

The Good Foods

A wholesome diet is not first-rate beneficial to your body; it will additionally provide you with a dramatic improvement on your intellectual performance.

Unsurprisingly, there also are nice food that could truely enhance your cognitive capability with everyday intake. Remember that the human mind, much like the relaxation of your inner organs, is depending for your nutrients. Certain factors also can lessen the cognitive decline in a person due to age.

Here is a list of the pinnacle 10 high-quality super factors:

Walnuts- Nuts and seeds are fantastic sources of nutrition E, which permits reduce the outcomes of cognitive decline as a person a while. Walnuts sell a wholesome blood and oxygen drift in someone's frame. A piece of walnut is also a reliable supply of ALA or alpha linolenic acid. It is essential for human development and boom. Other nuts and seeds together with cashews, peanuts, sunflower seeds, and sesame seeds also are feasible alternatives. Remember that it's far an lousy lot closing to eat unsalted nuts and get your every day sodium consumption from exceptional meals.

Blueberries – Blueberries are in particular effective in lessening the effects of cognitive decline due to developing vintage. It offers your mind resistance from oxidative strain, shielding you from positive neurological issues together with Alzheimer's ailment and dementia.

Coffee – Coffee beans are superb sources of caffeine; a wakefulness selling stimulant that offers a lift in alertness almost right away. Coffee is also has effective antioxidant homes, so they may be secure for every day intake. Remember that an excessive amount of coffee causes destructive consequences which encompass heartburn, insomnia, restlessness, and special signs and symptoms. Having 2 cups an afternoon is the maximum wholesome intake of espresso.

Whole Grains – Whole grains decorate the motion of blood and oxygen inside the path of the body collectively with the thoughts. Whole grains like brown rice, oatmeal, and wheat germ moreover drastically reduce the threat of developing cardiovascular illnesses. Frequent intake of complete grains moreover promotes higher physical metabolisms.

Dark Chocolate – Dark chocolate is an outstanding deliver of flavonoids and antioxidants. Dark chocolate consumption moreover lets in manipulate blood glide, blood pressure, and levels of cholesterol inside the blood. The caffeine found in dark chocolate is likewise an inexperienced wakefulness and application boosting agent. Lastly, all and sundry is keen on its wealthy flavour.

Fish – Omega-3 fatty acids with DHA (docosahexaenoic acid) make up approximately 60% of the mind. It is positioned in many bloodless-water fish meat which incorporates salmon, tuna, mackerel, herring, and halibut. Fish meat is also an tremendous deliver of herbal fish oil; a effective anti inflammatory agent essential for repairing cellular tissue. Eicospentaenoic acid or EPA, moreover observed in fish meat, improves the motion of blood and oxygen. Fish oil dietary supplements are being taken through way of patients with coronary heart conditions.

Tomato – Tomatoes and special red fruits and veggies along with watermelons and papayas are great sources of lycopene; an critical phytonutrient with powerful antioxidant houses. Lycopene is mainly effective in decreasing risks of coronary heart illnesses, macular degeneration, or even maximum cancers. A everyday consumption of tomato and tomato-primarily based meals protects the body from unfastened-radical harm to cells. It is effective in lowering the chance of growing cognitive decline in growing older human beings.

Sage – Sage is a culinary herb well-known for its numerous health blessings. It may be used to relieve not unusual illnesses inclusive of diarrhoea, heartburn, and flatulence. Sage is likewise used to help sufferers with melancholy, memory loss, and Alzheimer's disease.

Spinach – This inexperienced vegetable is an great deliver of lutein, eating regimen A, nutrients C, vitamins E, nutrients K, Omega-3 acids, and an entire lot of different vitamins which consist of folic acid. Lutein is an antioxidant powerful for lowering the outcomes of cognitive decline as someone a while. This consists of vision impairment and memory loss. The only hassle is that no longer all and sundry is eager on its flavor and culinary programs.

Apple – It is real that apples won't offer the superb thoughts-boosting talents, however it is one of the only and most reachable glowing end result you should buy almost everywhere. Apples protect the mind from neurodegenerative diseases together with

Alzheimer's disease and Parkinson's disease. Doctors say that ingesting apples help people think more truely while moreover enhancing their memory. Apples additionally contain vitamins that sell a median better health. But the brilliant detail about apples is their flavor and culinary packages.

Taking care of your thoughts with the useful resource of giving it right nourishment is one of the key steps in accomplishing advanced cognition. However, this doesn't constantly advise that you need to desert other meals types altogether. Having a healthy balanced diet plan remains greater important than having a weight-reduction plan targeted pleasant at the substances indexed above. Still, it is crucial to give emphasis in removing lousy food on the equal time as along with the tremendous factors.

Protein that comes from lean meat at the side of bird and lean pork cuts is likewise an essential nutrient for muscle increase and maintenance. It is also a supply of amino acids recognized to assemble resistance towards cognitive decline. There are also vegetarian protein resources which includes green peas, beans, tofu, and other veggies.

Also bear in mind that there can be an immediate courting amongst your physical and your highbrow health. Diversification is one of the first steps you need to take in case you need to regulate your manner of life proper into a greater thoughts-high-quality approach. It is time in case you want to be responsible for your non-public diet.

The mind is best greater or much less 2% of the whole body weight of a mean individual, but it makes use of up approximately 20% of energy consumed every day. The mind relies specifically on glucose, which may be metabolized from carbohydrates – on the entire from grains, fruits, and vegetables.

However, if the body is deprived of carbohydrates, the thoughts will then inn to wonderful substances for energy, specifically lactic acid or in reality lactate.

Lactate is the by-product of muscular tissues throughout difficult art work. Muscles rely specifically on glucose for energy, but it could furthermore reuse its non-public derivative (lactate) for strength. This concludes that the mind and your frame use the equal fuels if you need to feature well.

To end this bankruptcy, you need to observe everything you have got discovered about weight loss plan and its courting along with your mind into your lifestyle.

Basing from what you've got got learned from Foods to Avoid, emerge as aware about which of the dangerous meals kinds you consume greater frequently. Also determine the motives for this bad eating habit (art work, journey, and many others.). Using this facts, create your personal plan to avoid the ones food as an entire lot as possible.

From the list of the Good Foods, create and diversify a meal plan that you are inclined to maintain for weeks to return lower back. Do now not forget about about the importance of having a healthful, balanced weight loss plan. For your reference, the advocated each day consumption of energy is ,500 kcal for guys and 2,000 kcal for women. For proteins, an grownup guy need to get at the least fifty six grams an afternoon while an person lady have to get as a minimum forty six grams an afternoon.

Chapter 9: Methods to Improve Memory Performance

Link Method

The method includes relating to a chain of factors or duties that you need to bear in mind to a listing of "nexus" or linking terms which are simultaneously associated with some of from one to 10. This phrase of nexus acts as a hyperlink most of the huge variety and the data you want to learn or consider. For this purpose, this link word is also known as a clamp phrase.

To draw near the concept of this method, you need to be a infant once more. That is genuinely an instance of the way easy it is…. To a few quantity in which youngsters can observe it too.

The concept is to sequentially hyperlink the ones phrases or requirements which you need to keep in thoughts into agencies of . For our first instance, the ones are the terms we're going to hold in mind: light bulb, printer, giraffe, bottle and shopping cart.

Let us now sequentially hyperlink those phrases in pairs. When you link those terms, use humor, exaggeration, amount, size and movement to help make the relationship robust.

Bulb - Printer: You are that specialize in a big bulb for your tiny printer and it is so warmth that the printer begins offevolved to soften.

Printer - Giraffe: The tiny printer have been given trampled with the resource of manner of a giraffe who wasn't searching wherein he became going.

Giraffe - Bottle: The giraffe can be very thirsty and swallows the complete bottle of strawberry smoothie with the duvet and all.

Bottle - Shopping cart: The bottles had been in a buying cart that a person had forgotten inside the middle of the road.

Now, we've got were given our tale:

There modified right into a massive mild bulb internal a tiny printer. It shone very brightly and started out to make the printer to soften. Suddenly, a giraffe stepped onto the printer and ran away. After a few minutes, the giraffe felt worn-out and thirsty. It placed a bottle of strawberry smoothie internal an deserted buying cart within the center of a street. It swallowed the complete bottle in a single gulp...THE END.

Although it can appear long for a list of handiest 5 factors, if you try to memorize it or create your very personal, you'll be aware which you are capable of undergo in mind subjects right away with a piece of workout.

Exercises

Use the subsequent -word lists, link the terms in pairs after which increase to create a tale with them.

Listen - Pig; Talk - Food; Dancing - Stove; Young - Entrepreneur;

Family - Dog

Tree - Weapon; Respect - Hippopotamus; Queen - Air; Sea - Men;

Plane - Forest

***

Track Method

This technique makes use of gadgets to offer you a sign of what you need to undergo in mind. So, every time you notice that item, you may dig up exactly what you preferred to bear in mind whether or now not it's someone's name, avenue call, and plenty of others. Let's test the subsequent story.

Imagine a pair that has their house and they are used to unplugging the smartphone cord at night time time on every occasion they go to mattress. This manner, they avoid calls in the late-night time hours that would wake them up and disturb the tranquility in their sleep.

However, there may be a trouble proper right right here. Sometimes that the equal couple is looking for a name the subsequent morning and the mobile phone does not ring. What genuinely befell is they forgot to plug the cellphone over again in after they sooner or later awakened. People tried calling however the phone clearly did now not ring for apparent reasons.

One night time, one in each of them determined to knock over a chair inside the middle of the room. It turned into honestly consistent with the cellphone jack, looking from the entrance to the dwelling room. The plug became one and a 1/2 of meters within the again of.

The next morning, he can be the first to enter the residing room. As he approached thru the hall, he need to see the chair knocked over and at the back of it, he noticed the unplugged cable from the telephone. He right now remembered that he had accomplished that from the preceding night time. That's why the chair have become there: to help him don't forget and reconnect. That is the not unusual sense behind this particular technique.

The equal way it labored within the story, you could try making use of that logic for your life and watch the upgrades.

Exercise

Make a list of factors you have to do. According to the motive above, use some factor that offers you a sign to endure in mind what you need to do. When you get conversant within the ones, you may add greater subjects to consider.

***

Number-Rhyme Method

The rhymes and repetitions constitute techniques to beautify reminiscence. These techniques can artwork for absolutely everyone, no matter their memory degree.

Memorizing data using rhymes is each other manner you can short undergo in mind subjects whilst the state of affairs dreams it.

In fact, it actually works so nicely that humans have continued to apply it even after being a achievement with the first few attempts.

Start via way of searching out phrases that rhyme with numbers from one to ten or the times of the week, and memorize them. For example:

One - Anyone

Two - Zemstwo

Three - tree

Four - flour

Five - Dive

Let us say which you chose the following terms: Latvia, deltoids and cadmium. Start with primary. The clamp word is 'every body'. Imagine a guy named Anyone playing the tambourine below the balcony of his loved. Ensure which you visualize the scene in detail which includes the balcony, his face, his body, what he was wearing and the tambourine with the phrase Latvia embroidered on the tambourine.

Next, the clamp phrase for the variety is 'Zemstwo'. Imagine a statue of a person named Zemstwo that smokes a cigar. While the cloud of smoke comes from his mouth, it slowly office work the phrase deltoid. Repeat this approach with all of the numbers you need.

When you need to take into account a phrase, try to remember its variety. At that second, you may be surprised how brief you could endure in mind its clamp word. The photo will come in your memory and at the same time as you relive it, you may visualize the phrases hidden inside the tambourine, the smoke, and so on. The key is to visualize the scene in exquisite detail.

Exercise

Form rhymes the usage of phrases from that listing: Six-Seven-Eight-Nine-Ten-Eleven.

***

Number-Form Method

This approach could require you to anticipate matters or devices that look much like the form of numbers. It is a famous approach as it is straightforward to don't forget key photos. However, no variety is restricted to 1 item, ultimately growing your alternatives and adding range to make it less hard. Here are some primary thoughts of variety and form.

zero - It looks like a ball.

1 - It has the form of a pencil

2 - It can be a swan

three - On the aspect it suggests mountain or a clover leaf

four - It looks as if the sail of a deliver.

five - It might be a hook.

6 - It seems like a canon visible from in the back of.

7 - It might be a lamp publish

8 - It looks like a snowman.

9 - It may need to make you observed of a fern bud.

10 - Like a drum subsequent to a stick.

Here is a way to apply it. To keep in thoughts that Julius Caesar visited England in 55 BC you may visualize him coming into the u . S . A . With hooks (one below each arm) to represent the range fifty five. If you heard on the facts that the usa army price range rose 4 percent remaining 12 months, you could consider all the infantrymen, tanks and guns covered up internal a sailing deliver.

Your instructor says that absolute zero is equal to -273?, you could photo a swan illuminated by using a lamp put up subsequent to a giant clover leaf in a chilly wintry climate.

Practicing will will let you make your self acquainted with the crucial problem pics, however you can also find out one in all a kind shapes that may reason extra possibilities. The zero can represent something associated with sports activities in choice to being only a ball, while 1 can with out issue end up a pen, a broom, or a tube of ink, three can be a few issue from the sector and 4 can take a look at with an object, man or woman, movement or adjective related to the sea.

Exercises

Test your self. Could you use that device to don't forget the following?

The date of the number one motor flight: 1903

The morning convention time: 9:45

The form of sovereign states of Africa: fifty 4

***

Letter-Shape Method

Similar to the technique above, the letter-form method adopts the identical manner to memorize the letters. You can companion the letters from A to Z with subjects that have the same or similar shape to the letter.

After making this connection, you could start to link the context with the object. Feel unfastened to get innovative make your non-public list. Here are a few mind of letters and shapes that get you off to an notable start:

A: mountain, a couple of compasses, image of warning...

B: a pregnant lady, seagull with outstretched wings, a brassiere...

C: vicinity moon, scythe, sickle...

...

Z: a bolt of lightning, avenue with curves...

Here is an example of the manner to exercise this technique. Let's don't forget phrases that you want to maintain in thoughts consisting of ball, book, and dog. Link the letters with the standards to go through in thoughts the use of humor, exaggeration, amount, period and movement.

A: a couple of compasses - ball: You try to draw a ball that's the scale of a single chickpea with a compass that is ten meters tall.

B: seagull - ebook: Imagine a seagull with glasses sitting subsequent to a hearth analyzing a ebook.

C: area moon - canine: An massive canine took a piece out of the moon and left handiest 1 / 4.

Exercise

Find some concepts which you need to hold in thoughts. Associate the letters from A to Z with subjects that might have a similar form to the letter.

Try to maintain in thoughts the ones devices of phrases:

Cat, banana, television, potato chips, handphone.

Cupboard, glass, residence, park, umbrella.

***

First letter approach

This technique is likewise called the mnemonics approach. It is a completely useful and traditional manner to recollect short texts which can be commonly utilized in college. It basically consists of writing the number one letter of every word of the text that you want to memorize, forming an extended line of nonsensical letters. Then you need to create a random sentence through using the first letters as your new terms.

Let us try and recall the order of our sun device planets as an instance (Mercury, Venus, Earth, Mars, Jupiter, Saturn, Uranus, Neptune, Pluto). By the usage of best the first letter, we've got M V E M J S U N P. Now, allow's try to create a sentence which isn't always related to the proper context. This is probably my version: My Very Enthusiastic Mother Just Sent Us Nine Potatoes.

Of route, you may have a have a observe the text each time you want it but the trick is to workout as plenty as feasible. By guiding your self with the letters, you teach the reminiscence to preserve the facts efficiently.

This will assist you will store statistics for your short-time period memory and with non-save you workout, you will word that it will ultimately be stored within the extended-time period reminiscence. As you enhance, you will observe that you handiest want to look the road of letters with a purpose to recite the entire text.

Exercise

Try the use of the mnemonics method to do not forget those terms:

Red, Orange, Yellow, Blue, Indigo, Violet.

***

Short text the use of be aware-taking

To begin memorizing a text, you need to relax and supply your self time. Start with any brief text of approximately one hundred and fifty terms. The perfect situation might be to copy and rewrite the textual content on some different paper. Why? Because at the same time as you write it, your mind cells are recording the motion and searching for to repair it into your reminiscence. Once you're completed writing, observe it aloud and in case you stuck on fast, you could flow into immediately to an prolonged textual content. If no longer, a few other trick is to put in writing down the textual content and divide it into quick sentences.

The concept is to recite the number one written phrase in a noisy voice, then combine it with the second one. Once you've got determined them, you will integrate the primary with the second one, then 2nd with the 0.33. Eventually, you could understand the textual content via coronary heart. This tactic very powerful for brief texts due to the fact with longer texts it may be a bit more tough. Let us test out a number of those longer ones.

Tips for word-taking

#1: Write inside the margins

Some human beings thing out the phrases which is probably maximum tough for them to memorize so after they see them, they're capable of take into account the complete text.

#2: Point out the maximum critical phrases (key phrases)

Try to take a look at a few of the strains of the paragraph to turn out to be aware about keywords that summarize the paragraph, and deliver a stylish idea of what is being cited.

#three: Underlining with hues

Colors can assist make the memorizing manner less complex due to the fact the brain may be very receptive to colour variations. If you do now not want to underline with many colours, use handiest purple or yellow. However, you need to undergo in thoughts that if too many colours are used the mind now not treats it as a warning and it's going to no longer have any which means.

***

Some carrying events to exercising

Exercise #1

Try to do not forget the times of the week in alphabetical order. Recite it aloud. Record the time it took at the manner to do not forget it. The shorter the time, the higher the cease end result. Try to apply the strategies you have were given found out previously.

Exercise #2

Try to recite the months of the one year in alphabetical order. After you are finished, try and do it the alternative manner round, reversing the alphabetical order.

Exercise #3

Add the sum of your date of shipping as visible right here: mm + dd + yyyy. It's going to provide you a number of that you need to hold in mind and recite aloud. Do the identical with the date of starting of your buddies and circle of relatives. Record the time it took that allows you to recollect it.

Exercise # 4

Name objects for each letter of your first name. You can strive starting with six items, but this all is based upon on how many you may find out that begin with the number one letter of your first name. Now, try to memorize all the names of those gadgets without looking at what you wrote. As you get higher at it, you may increase the wide variety of letters and items.

Exercise # five

Wherever you are, truely take about 2 mins to appearance all spherical you. Try to find out five small things that in shape on your pocket and five massive topics which can be too massive to wholesome. Try to do not forget their names without searching at them.

If you need to be properly-rounded on this experience, it's miles encouraged which you use numerous techniques in combination because of the fact quality education one of the strategies will no longer be enough to obtain your intention.

If you need to check and memorize brief in order that it remains for your reminiscence, there a few the ones techniques and approaches that we're capable of be searching at on this next bankruptcy that you can discover quite useful.

Chapter 10: Advanced techniques to teach your approach

Concentration is the functionality to recovery our interest voluntarily and sustained in a particular discipline or fabric. In this number one economic catastrophe of our eBook, we're going to suggest a few techniques of attention that can help you enhance your ability to cognizance or concentrate, with special emphasis on elements that without delay have an effect on hobby.

Attention is essential in nearly any issue of our existence and especially in gaining knowledge of and examine. We can learn how to enhance our interest:

Generating the situations and moves that propitiate it

Eliminating conditions and distracting factors

The workout of cognizance need to be achieved every on the tune (or in which the hobby takes vicinity) and outside. Like physical abilities, interest is a highbrow ability that want to be practiced to beautify it. One of the first rate techniques to practice attention is to make sure that the individual concentrates properly (and is taken appreciably) in the direction of the training classes.

To offer an example, and even though it appears stupid, if it is been scientifically showed that the presence of the overall public, their moods and screams have an impact at the overall performance of athletes, why no longer exercising throwing a penalty (or every exceptional interest) with the Same screaming?

Developing key phrases that can be used throughout education, play or competitive situations may be very beneficial to direct the awareness approach.

1-. Conditions and actions that sell hobby:

1-Set desires and desires

The putting of properly-described desires assist you to pretty to pay attention. If you've got got a large task in mind or a topic with a very huge time table, you could enhance your hobby in case you divide the work into smaller dreams and extra potential objectives.

People, as a extremely-contemporary rule, we can not repair our attention on more than 7 elements of facts at a time. Therefore if we divide our venture or have a observe into smaller quantities and attack every piece one after the other it'll be a remarkable deal plenty much less tough to enhance our interest thinking about the truth that we reputation our interest on a unmarried detail.

2-Do only one challenge at a time

From the hand of the preceding element, do an ant artwork and commit your self to a unmarried challenge and your hobby will now not range inflicting you to lose cognizance.

three-Limit time

If you want to expand a undertaking in your artwork or beauty for that you are given a duration of 24 hours, the fast time will strain you to pay attention on its execution and you could focus satisfactory on the necessities. If you're given consistent with week for the equal mission, there can be 7 days of extra factors and filling time. If you get months, you turns into a highbrow vampire with 60 days to suck your blood. Self-enforcing time limitations on every responsibilities and small duties are essential to maintaining your consciousness.

four-Generate hobby

Interest is one of the important factors that can help you cognizance your hobby. We be privy to what interests us and additionally with very little attempt. If you get interested by a topic it will be less complicated to awareness your hobby on it and observe it greater without issue. But now a few different query arises: how can you are making your self interested by some thing that truly does no longer hobby you? Well, right here are a few highbrow strategies that serve to accumulate this aim:

Link the advantages that you are going to achieve to recognition attention on a have a study situation matter with that same problem of have a have a look at. That is, constantly preserve in thoughts that listening to a selected hassle will convey you future advantages.

Leverage elements that appeal to your interest and channel it towards those elements wherein it prices you greater to pay attention. You're going to do intellectual Aikido.

For instance, when you have established a few goals for a challenge or undertaking and you've got were given completed a time trouble, you could cognizance your attention on improving the time that you have imposed to carry out this mission, you may additionally reputation your interest on doing it more efficiently and beauty.

Anyway, you'll collaterally get your interest centered on the project with the aid of using way of leveraging the time quandary, the undertaking of enhancing it sluggish or the aim to do higher.

five-Self-regulate

It is critical to test periodically if the techniques used are walking or not. You can analyze in what moments you've got got been greater focused and what you have got finished concretely to advantage this u . S . Of concentration. You also can examine the instances wherein it's been extra hard if you need to concentrate and try to decide the factors that have led you to that loss of attention.

2-. Main distractors that you could discover

Disorder and chaos

It may be of types: outside and inner.

1-External chaos

It is what we've in our artwork or take a look at surroundings. If you've got got a messy environment it's going to probable be more difficult to pick interest and until you do now not remedy it you may be curtailing that functionality that you want a lot. Some movements that you may take in order that the sickness can not be with you:

Take an inventory of those likely distracting outdoor elements and fasten them one after the opportunity. Some elements that you can endure in mind are the subsequent in 10 mins:

Order your paintings surroundings.

Free region for your desk: Leave exceptional the necessities to artwork and the relaxation make it disappear from your sight.

Outside alarms of cellular telephones and virtual devices

If you parent with the laptop, flip off the alarms of the emails and near all the ones pages which you do now not need and which could distract you.

Stay a ways from paintings or vampiric care buddies or growth techniques to keep them at bay.

2-Internal chaos

It takes place whilst we've got were given too many responsibilities in our heads that distract our interest from the reason we should gain. To some quantity, our mind is constantly reminding us that we must do some element and that we cannot overlook it.

An powerful way to sell off your thoughts simply so it could lighten up and deliver attention to the present day task; it is to materialize in a listing on paper, all the ones elements which is probably there and attract your interest. To positioned it in a slightly crude way, it's miles like throwing up your complete intellectual load on that listing. Once you have completed it and on the time you bear in mind suitable, you may manner that list in order and you can make a preference approximately what to do with each element.

3-Training

These principles ought to examine and located into exercise. If you suggest to consist of them grade by grade into your have a look at and paintings sporting events, you'll recognize that your hobby and attention improves. It is useless to apprehend those necessities if you do now not execute them and placed them into workout, so we encourage you to use them on your studies and paintings.

10 Exercises to mastering your intellectual focus

Exercise #1: Counting phrases

Get a text; it could be the internet internet web page of a ebook or a magazine. Mind mentally in order that it includes the primary paragraph. Then, count number huge range the second. And so on. Try now not to apply your finger or specific assist to guide you; use exquisite the eyes. As it fees you plenty less art work, try and consider all of the phrases on a web page.

Exercise # 2: Numbers in the head

Close your eyes. You are going to count to 100 or as an awful lot as the amount you get inside the following manner:

Imagine the photograph of #1 and say your name mentally.

Then, make it fade absolutely so the amount 2 appears in your head as even though they had been slides.

Say .

The 2 is going away. The three appears...

And maintain like this until the end of the exercising.

You can also rely backward (a hundred, ninety nine, 98 ...). How is it going?

Exercise # three: Walking

Walking improves interest, but you could also educate it with this workout, which is likewise to anticipate.

Count 5 steps (1, 2, 3, four, and 5).

To the subsequent step, begin from the beginning, however accomplishing up to six

The next, start from the start and reaches 7

Continue like this until you reap 10

Then, rely decrease lower back nice 5

Repeat the complete series as typically as you need.

Exercise # four: Walk quietly spherical

Walk round, ideally a park or some other area wherein exceptional scents converge. Focus on what number of unique smells you can stumble on. Identify them and then stay with the simplest you need outstanding approximately them. Concentrate on my own on that. You may be aware that the aroma that you have chosen intensifies because of the eye you placed on it.

Exercise # five: That spot on the wall

Take a sit down. Look on the wall and take your eyes to three unique element (a few spot, hollow or comparable). Keep your eyes there, but concentrate as a whole lot as you may to your respiration; how the air slowly enters the lungs and the way it is coming out later.

Exercise # 6: Quiet because of the fact the chair

Sit in a cushty chair; now not in more, it'll likely be which you fall asleep. Your challenge can be to live though, very quiet. It isn't always as clean as it seems. Relax, attention and attempt not to make any involuntary motion. Do you preserve five minutes? With a piece exercise, you'll reach 15. This is a few one of a kind brilliant exercise to loosen up.

Exercise # 7: Mental images

Choose an item from the ones round you; this is, a pen, a cup ... And take a couple of minutes to examine it carefully. Think about its shape, its coloration, the substances it is made with, and so forth. Try to take a image together together with your thoughts. Then, near your eyes and try to recreate that item to your head with as many facts as you may.

Exercise # 8: A sound that occupies the whole thing

Choose a word or a legitimate; a mantra, as an example, or what making a decision upon. Repeat it mentally, flippantly, with out thinking about some thing else for 5 minutes. You will increase the notice-time while you're loose.

Exercise # 9: One concept and go away the rest

Of all of the thoughts that move your thoughts, pick out one; ideally splendid, and dedicate your self to explore it for a few minutes, without thinking about a few issue else.

Here it might be exceptional, for instance, to practice that exercising of gratitude.

We summarize it:

Think of a time even as some element accurate passed off and you felt nicely; for example, the tranquility that you felt even as you noticed dawn this morning.

Recreate that 2d in your thoughts with as many facts as you can. Revive it.

Focus on the extraordinary sensations of the immediately. Walk via it. Intensify them.

As you find out it less complicated, the attention-time will growth.

Exercise # 10: Relax earlier than going to sleep

Fill a pitcher of water and region it at the bedside desk. Sit in front of it have a have a look at it. Try to think handiest about the water, how easy and quiet it's miles. Recreate that peace in you. Imagine your self so calm and you will see that, in a very short time, the tensions and twitches provide way to a totally fine u . S . A . Of relaxation that could make your dream a whole lot less tough.

Close your eyes and skip lower back mentally; remembering everything you have got finished at a few stage inside the day. Try to rescue all of the records you can. Practice the sporting sports and strategies which you much like the maximum and revel in its advantages.

Chapter 11: Increase your chances of achievement through putting dreams

"Setting dreams is the first step in turning the invisible worldwide into the visible" - Tony Robbins

"People with dreams achieve success due to the fact they recognise in which they'll be going." - Earl Nightingale

For most of my individual existence, I even have had the delight of summers off from university. It is a present that I don't take as a right. When my kids were growing vintage my partner came up with a exceptional concept. She endorsed that everyone write down three subjects they favored to do all through the summer season excursion. We all wrote down our three gadgets after which combined them proper proper into a summer time listing of things to do, like a summer time "bucket list". As quick as university changed into out we commenced running on our listing of factors to get completed in the summer season. By the cease of summer time, we had performed most of the list. We also decided some thing essential: You can get loads extra achieved through writing down what you need to do and attention in this list.

During university, I certainly loved the usage of bicycles. I take into account going to the library and studying Bicycle mag. In the magazine, I observed masses of articles and images of Italian racing bicycles. I owned a totally reasonably-priced 10-tempo motorcycle from K-Mart and I wanted an decorate. I walked proper into a network motorbike hold and noticed a completely cool Italian racing motorbike hooked up at the wall. I HAD to have this motorbike. I had one moderate problem: a very restrained fee range. What I did become something I've best completed a handful of instances at some point of my existence, however I informed myself I become going to have this new bike irrespective of what. Looking all over again, it was as though I willed the bike to myself. I went domestic and got to work. I offered a few stuff, did abnormal jobs, offered extra stuff, and decrease grass. I have become so focused not anything may additionally need to stop me from getting that motorcycle. It took me about 8 weeks to keep up for the motorcycle however I can nevertheless bear in mind the day as quickly as I wheeled the motorcycle domestic. I rode the bike to highschool every day for the relaxation of college, after which for 3 greater years after graduating. I cherished each 2nd of using it. From looking for the brilliant new bike I observed out the electricity of reason placing and attention.

The method of setting goals is quite smooth.

? Take a while to mirror on what you would really like to carry out.

? Write the ones goals down and positioned a date to carry out them.

? Check at the goals often.

? Take movement that allows you to accomplish the motive.

Goals are powerful because they help you interest on what you need to carry out in life. Please don't have the phantasm that by using the use of writing down dreams they mechanically are going to take vicinity. Writing down the desires is the first step and you then virtually virtually need to be follow up through manner of taking movement.

As you observe the subsequent testimonies approximately folks that wrote down excellent dreams after which performed them, you will be conscious that that they had a dream, wrote it down, and then took movement to carry out their intention. The first story comes from absolutely one in all my preferred books Running with the Buffaloes by means of manner of manner of Chris Lear. The author decided the University of Colorado move the usa of america organization for an entire season and wrote approximately it. The movie celebrity of the crew grow to be Adam Goucher. He became the fantastic runner at his excessive college, however he favored greater. He wrote down 4 goals on a poster board that he hung in his room. The four dreams were

1. Win the kingdom championship

2. Win Footlocker Midwest

3. Win Footlocker National Championship

four. Long Term-Collegiate National Champion, Make Olympic Team

His educate defined how he often had to run by way of using way of himself because no character want to maintain up with him, but he by no means complained. Before the Midwest race, there was a snowstorm, however he changed into even though out education in the extreme, frigid climate. During university, he ran very early within the morning to get in his miles. He possessed a robust desire to perform his desires and have become willing to artwork for them. In the surrender, he modified into capable to perform each one in each of his dreams. He changed right into a -time Colorado excessive university america champion, Footlocker national champion his senior three hundred and sixty five days, NCAA country wide champion in university, and -time Olympic enterprise member. All four of those lofty goals Goucher wrote at the poster in his youth room got here real together along along with his talents and tough artwork.

Jack Canfield is a international magnificence speaker and coauthor of the well-known e-book collection, "Chicken Soup for the Soul." Although the collection has bought loads of masses of copies, the ebook have become clearly an idea at one time. Jack Canfield has a intention of promoting 1.Five million copies via using December 30, 1994. His wrote the aim down on a enterprise card and carried this in his wallet. In addition, he vowed to do 5 subjects every day to assist sell the e book. By the aim date, he had supplied 1.Three million books.

John Grisham has supplied over 250 million books. His first ebook A Time to Kill changed into inspired via paying attention to the tale a twelve-3 hundred and sixty five days-antique lady knowledgeable to a jury. He went domestic that night time and started out writing his first ebook. He set a purpose of growing each morning at 5 am and writing at least one net web page. He caught along together with his each day motive and have become capable of write a ebook even as running complete-time as an criminal expert. If he had now not set this reason he might also additionally moreover have by no means finished his first ebook and grow to be a famous creator.

When John Goddard modified into 15 years he wrote down a listing of 127 dreams he would like to perform in his lifetime. Many of the goals had been very ambitious, like going to the moon or circumventing the arena. But he figured that if he accomplished all of his dreams he can also need to have had a lifestyles of adventure and belief. After writing out the list he did some component that maximum humans fail to do; he took movement. The very subsequent day he started taking steps to carry out his listing of desires. Before his dying, he became succesful to carry out over ninety% of those existence dreams.

Urban Myer is a college soccer educate. Through his profession, he has received 3 national championships, a feat only a few coaches had finished. However, after triumphing his 2nd National Championship he became about as miserable as someone can be. He became confused, in unwell health, and had not noted his own family through focusing handiest on soccer. He knew his lifestyles have become out of stability, so he quit training to recognition on his family. Without the stress of education, he turned into able to attend his youngsters's wearing events and abilties. He loved being a exceptional father. After years of not training, Ohio State contacted him about a activity. He desired to head lower back to schooling but furthermore wanted to be an outstanding father. His 3 youngsters had an idea. They wrote out eleven goals for him to decide to in advance than returning to training. The desires worried attending their activities, taking day off on the weekend, and now not being an absent father. He made the willpower to perform the eleven dreams and decrease returned to education. Now even as considered one of his children has a wearing event, he stops his work and attends the occasion. He not works all weekend and sees his family. What he placed is that he may be a in reality proper educate and a incredible father. The desires have given him path in his lifestyles.

When you write goals down and determine to accomplishing them, you deliver your thoughts route and reputation.

Bob Frapples loved studying motivational books. His favourite creator have become Jack Canfield. In his e-book, The Success Habits Jack Cranfield counseled that you need to write down down one hundred dreams you would like to perform on your lifetime. This concept inspired Bob to put in writing down down down his listing of a hundred desires. One of his dreams have grow to be to meet Jack Canfield and characteristic a communication with him. At this detail Bob had completed step one of task goals: he had written the reason down. Many human beings prevent right right here and definitely start wishing. What occurred subsequent is a top notch example of the strength of writing down goals and then taking motion. Bob observed on Mr. Canfield's internet site that he end up talking in his location of basis in a few weeks. He notion that this could be an possibility to fulfill him. He provided tickets and went to the event. After Mr. Canfield spoke Bob idea he can also need to go down and meet him. However, many human beings had the identical idea. Bob waited and waited patiently and ultimately had been given the braveness to attempt to talk to him. As he went as an entire lot as Mr. Canfield the subsequent speaker got here on degree and Bob started out looking for a seat. By risk there was an open seat proper next to Mr. Canfield, so Bob sat down. For the subsequent hours, he grow to be able to talk with Jack Canfield among audio machine and they in the long run have become pals. Amazing subjects will take region in case you set a cause and begin taking movement to accumulate the ones dreams.

You're in no way too more youthful to start writing down and reaching desires. Create a list of a hundred gadgets you would like to perform. Dream massive after which begin taking movement closer to the ones desires. For instance, Taylor Swift had the dream of turning into a rustic singer. She changed into capable of persuade her mother and father to transport to Nashville to pursue her cause. If you don't have dreams and course in life, than exclusive humans will set your desires for you. You'll turn out to be the worker for the boss.

If you could define the WHY, then you could parent out the HOW.

When I became in immoderate university I had a friend who had already figured out what he desired to do in lifestyles. His name became Michael and he wanted to be a medical health practitioner. I do not forget him telling every body about looking for to be a doctor in a few unspecified time inside the future of our freshman twelve months in excessive faculty. I didn't have any concept what I preferred to do later in lifestyles. I figured you need to go to university, however I didn't clearly have any purpose for faculty. Michael knew he wished unique grades in excessive college and university at the manner to get into medical faculty. He had a "why" related to his college and motivation to do properly. Not for his mother and father, but for his destiny profession. I was a very common pupil in high university. But once I arrived in university I figured what I did now would possibly effect my picks later in life. I now had purpose connected to my studies. I made plenty higher grades in university than in immoderate college.Discovering your "why" will assist you spot the favored paintings as a stepping stone to in that you need to be. I heard a tale currently that illustrates my aspect.

Kimanzi Constable grew up in Milwaukee, Wisconsin. After high college he were given a manner riding a bread truck. He preferred the system and worked from nighttime to six within the morning. Life became specific. After severa years of the usage of the truck he had been given married after which kids got here alongside. One day he awoke and positioned out he hated using the bread truck. He felt caught in a activity he hated and figured he had no different alternatives aside from using the truck. While the use of one night time time he listened to a podcast approximately an writer who wrote ebooks. As crazy because it seemed, Kimanzi belief he want to perhaps do the identical. He started out out writing approximately his lifestyles as a bread truck driving force and what he observed at night time at the same time as others slept. He wrote his ebook, posted it on Amazon, and waited for his cash to roll in. But after weeks he had a trouble; he had now not supplied a unmarried ebook. He desired to forestall and started out to doubt himself. However, he saved thinking about his "why" and that he have become going to write down a success ebooks. He spent a year promoting his ebook and inspecting how others provided their ebooks on line. He worked tirelessly on promoting the e-book and wrote the second. He stored thinking "If I can efficaciously write and market ebooks, I can prevent the usage of a bread truck". There had been regularly on the same time as he felt discouraged, but he saved remembering why he wanted to write and positioned up an ebook in the first location. Two years after writing his first ebook, the sales began out coming in and he supplied 10,000 copies of his first books. This unfold out greater opportunities and he ultimately had been given a settlement with a publishing organisation to install writing down four hardcover books. Just three years after identifying his "why" and writing his first e-book, Kimanzi has stopped the use of a bread truck and runs an online eBook commercial enterprise organization at the aspect of getting many talking opportunities. He moved from Wisconsin to Hawaii. When you can determine out your "why", you may locate the motivation to perform your intention.

Summary Points

? Writing down goals help via providing you with course and focus in existence.

? Create a list of 100 lifestyles dreams

? Discovering your "why" will assist you be successful and triumph over hard instances.

How should you're taking notes?

We all have our very very own fashion and persona. I may advise that you take notes in a format that works incredible for you. I will offer 3 options and use the style which you like super. These techniques can be used for taking notes in beauty, reading from the textbook, or looking films. Taking proper notes and retaining them organized can save you a exquisite quantity of time while analyzing for the take a look at.

Good conduct for be conscious taking:

? Always name your notes and include a date, web page range (if it is from a textual content), and situation remember.

? Keep the notes multi function binder, spiral pocket ebook, or composition pocket book. Never have the notes on free quantities of paper. This is a recipe for disorganized notes.

? Use shade on the side of your notes. You can spotlight titles in a single coloration and definitions in every unique.

? Symbols can also be beneficial.

For instance, use a bullet for everyday information.

An arrow for consequences or effects.

A subject for examples.

My desired approach of phrase taking is the Cornell examine taking technique. The

Cornell method became advanced in 1949 at Cornell University by using Walter Paulk. It has been used successfully via the usage of college students for decades. I pick out Cornell notes due to the reality, at the same time as completed nicely, it gives a layout that you could use later for remember and is simple to create quizzes from.

Cornell Notes:

Step 1. Set up your notes in the Cornell phrase taking format by using folding your

paper into thirds, developing columns.

In addition, depart place on the top and the bottom of the paper.

Picture of Cornell Notes: see next web web page

You can get a reproduction of a clean Cornell Notes at this hyperlink:

http://englishlinx.Com/reading_comprehen sion/cornell-notes-studying-comprehension.Html

Step 2. In the pinnacle phase call the notes, write the date, and every different data so you can help whilst reading for the check.

Step 3. In the right column write notes from the e-book, lecture, or video. The notes may be in bullet form, statements, or any format you pick. You can upload pics, charts, or some thing else so you can help. You may even doodle on this segment. In truth, research has tested that doodling can increase keep in mind later.

Step four. In the left columns write titles for the notes you wrote. The titles have to be quick summaries or descriptions of what you wrote inside the notes section.

Step five. You can be tempted to pass this ultimate section, but it is able to be very beneficial in studying the cloth. At the bottom phase, you could summarize the notes. The act of summarizing allows the thoughts internalize the notes and will increase don't forget.

Outline technique:

Another technique of be conscious taking is to create outlines of what you're studying or taking note of. This method can be difficult finally of a lecture however may be very powerful with a textbook. The gain is that an outline permits you to condense new cloth into one record that you may look over short.

Here is an example of an define layout of notes:

Let's say the ones notes were for a check on Tuesday over 4 of the "musical time durations." Your fundamental subject matter, 4 time intervals, is farthest to the left on the pinnacle of the web page. Below is the primary time period, Medieval. And underneath that is records about it. Main subjects are up the front and information is underneath. It is pretty simple, however makes the statistics organized and easy to appearance over. Also, you could spotlight your vital difficulty remember quantity, subtopics, and key dates.

Mind Maps or Graphic Organizers

Another technique of note taking is developing mind maps or photograph organizers. One manner to create a mind map is to attract a circle and write the problem call inner it. Next, draw spokes from the circle if you want to give an explanation for sub-topics. At the quit of the spoke, you could write an define or draw a photograph. Here is an instance of several thoughts maps.

A mind map allows you to be modern and gives a visual picture. You can area timelines or charts for your mind maps.

Videos on a way to create a mindmap:

Mind Map Tutorial

https://www.Youtube.Com/watch?V=tAUsZ 9eiorY

How to use thoughts maps for analyzing

https://www.Youtube.Com/watch?V=PxwYc W3E5Mw

Summary notes

? Start getting geared up for assessments early. This sounds easy, however most college students wait until the very last second.

? Actively compare your notes through growing check questions, summaries, or outlines of the notes.

? Before you dive into your take a look at steerage, try to discern out wherein your instructor will pull take a look at questions from. Ask yourself, "will my trainer ask questions from my notes, the ebook, or the have a observe manual." Then format your have a look at time throughout the most vital regions.

? Learn to take tremendous notes. Pick a style of notes that you revel in.

? Cornell notes, an outline, or a mind map are three methods you can take notes.

Chapter 12: 7 Quickest Ways to Make You a Faster Learner

Winning is constantly relying on your functionality to take a look at. The quicker you studies, the higher the achievements you will get. This easy rule defines academic success.

But the reading approach can be difficult to maximum people particularly college college students. Many university college students battle throughout their stay in school. In truth, some have given up and determined any other way of surviving lifestyles other than obtaining an academic degree.

However, the hassle isn't always the lack of belongings or private talents to check. Most college university students apprehend the educational worldwide the wrong way.

And the purpose why they locate it tough reading their lessons is their way of dealing with educational art work. Of direction, getting to know includes preserving as many records as feasible. But you can't acquire it with out effective techniques.

Faster learner college students do nicely in college now not due to the reality they have got a excessive IQ; they'll be actually proper at gaining knowledge of effective techniques in studying. The following guidelines allow you to reap educational fulfillment too.

1. Understand what sort of learner you're

The problem of most university students is that they do not know what sort of learner they may be. Different people have one-of-a-type styles of analyzing.

For example, a few college college students undergo in mind nicely what they test after they concentrate to tune. They belong to an auditory learner beauty. If this is authentic to you, can be, you may encompass music into your look at behavior. So each time you vicinity your self to check, play a song which you love that will help you apprehend the trouble better.

If you're an auditory learner, why not record the elegance discussions and play them at the same time as you take a look at rather than studying your notes? Your cellphone may be beneficial in recording the lectures.

The 2d type is a visible content material fabric cloth learner. Students who're content material learner normally commonly generally tend to examine efficiently at the same time as the substances are entire of pix, charts, graphs, flashcards, and plenty of others.

If you are this sort of learner then transform your lectures into pix. Use graphs and flash playing playing cards to aid your getting to know.

The ultimate kind is the physical learner. People who belong to this elegance love doing a little issue even as analyzing. Students who are bodily beginners determined it much less hard to go through in thoughts the lecture on the same time as tapping their ft or gambling with their pen.

Small bodily movement allows them emerge as a quicker learner.

2. Use on line gear

Technology, if used well, might also want to make a distinction to your existence. Having said this, you may take gain of on-line equipment. There are net web sites on the way to assist you to make flashcards. The StudyBule is one in every of them.

The PaperGear is some other on-line tool you may use to assist the brainstorming approach much less complex. Lastly, if you're searching out strategies to make complex topics much less complicated, use Brainscape. Using the ones system make your check durations powerful.

three. Be willing to simply accept new statistics

It takes masses of motivation to truly begin studying. As a cease end result, many college college students emerge as procrastinating.

But a short learner student has his/her very very own manner of making topics going. However, it wishes a hint intellectual education to increase interest. And one manner to advantage this is with the aid of the usage of beginning your mind to new ideas. Once you have were given an open mind, you will get passionate about the subject. The extra you switch out to be excited, the more you becomes an eager and faster learner.

4. Find a conducive region to take a look at

Clearly, you can not popularity analyzing in a distractive location. The reason is that your thoughts cannot perform multitasking consisting of attending to external stimuli (noises) at the same time as analyzing.

If you need to become a faster learner, you need to detach from social interactions. Well, this doesn't mean that you have to be delinquent. Of route, you want pals. But if you cannot deal with your examine due to their presence, you need to discover a quiet region.

5. Construct maps for your thoughts

Learning is all approximately making mind maps. Visual representations can be effective in making your take a look at much less complicated. One way to do it's far to make symbols associated with the facts you need to maintain in thoughts. Connect all of the information together as though they're part of a puzzle. This manner permits you to take a look at speedy.

6. Find the super memorization approach that fits you

There are many techniques to memorize facts very results. However, no longer all of them are relevant to anyone. Some humans are effective whilst memorizing the complete sentence, at the same time as others are cushty in memorizing word via word.

But memorizing without statistics can be useless. So you want to discover your very personal manner to bind memorization and know-how collectively. Just take a look at what technique fits you the most.

7. Study regularly

If you need to be a faster learner, you need to take an additional mile. Achieving immoderate educational grades include a awesome quantity of hard work. That's the truth. If you do not push your self, you may advantage nothing each in faculty and in actual life.

Regular reading additionally helps you set up the neural connection of your mind so one can maintain the records. It's like bodily exercise. The extra you have interaction in it, the greater you emerge as stronger.

In addition, the more potent neural connection makes it less complicated that allows you to keep the data for an prolonged term. Above all, normal observe conduct allow you to keep away from cramming.

6 Habits of Straight-A Students

Most university students battle at university. As a instructor, I see a majority of university college students fail and feature troubles with their courses.

On the opportunity thing, there quite a few who surely succeeded in accomplishing excessive grades. So the essential question is: what separates a few pretty a fulfillment university university college students from the bulk who fail?

Of route, you may argue that intelligence is one big aspect in educational success. But it isn't continuously the case. In reality, now not all proper away-A college students have excessive IQ.

However, while you have got a take a look at highly a fulfillment college university college students, you'll get a clean idea what makes them a success. Generally, the common component that defines instructional success is a dependancy.

Like in real existence, behavior play critical position in reaching desires. Good behavior reason excessive success. And the terrible conduct will cause horrible and unwanted effects. Here are the 8 conduct which is probably commonplace among mainly a success university students.

1. Straight-A scholar plans ahead

If you're a scholar, try to study what your fellow college college students are doing. Chances are you'll take a look at that a lot of them (may additionally additionally moreover encompass yourself) spend loads time speaking topics that aren't related to their educational topics.

That's the not unusual scenario. Have you determined a single pupil who stays in one nook analyzing a e-book? I wager, you may't continuously see a student like that? Why? Because they are unusual.

But what makes a success college students one in all a kind? Why are they appear like so busy all the time? Well, it is due to the truth they don't waste their time doing unproductive sports activities activities.

They commonly make plans. They comply with schedules for all in their sports activities. Observing time is part of their dependancy.

Whereas the majority of college college students certainly roam round with out purpose. They don't be aware of their schedules. As a stop result, they emerge as cramming when the final examination and reduce-off date come.

Academic achievement consists of planning ahead of time. It lets in you to monitor how thousands you've performed already and what type of paintings left to be accomplished.

If you need to be a right away-A scholar, a list of sports activities and a calendar are your vital equipment. Observe time carefully and follow schedules strictly.

But this doesn't suggest that you must neglect all of your pals and loved ones. A a hit student is properly-rounded. This technique that s/he can do different extracurricular sports too. When you observe your plans properly, you'll have greater unfastened time to spend with unique sports.

Through beautify making plans, you could gather more success.

2. Straight-A scholar rapid adapts maturity

Another first-rate or addiction of a success college students is that they may be flexible to growth. They make their very own options and they do their stuff independently. This is a sign that they get older. In different phrases, they discover ways to emerge as responsible for their actions.

Growing older isn't constantly associated with chronological age. It's extra of a intellectual age. In reality, some kids have better choice-making functionality than adults.

Being a student, there's a massive opportunity which you live in an rental away from domestic. You put together dinner your very own food, wash your non-public clothes, and buy your food substances. It can be frightening before the whole lot. But if you may be capable of adapt to the trendy surroundings and new existence fashion, you'll effortlessly get used to it.

three. Straight-A student solves his/her own troubles

Highly a fulfillment college students discover solutions for his or her issues. They significantly find out methods to treatment the impediment.

However, they don't try to be immodest with the aid of way of not asking help. Of direction, they need guidelines and assist from others. In fact, locating assist from special people is an indication of intelligence.

What a hit students do is that they will attempt to discern out the manner to remedy a trouble on hand first. Some groups name this the 15-minute rule. What this suggests is that, if you come across a difficult trouble, do not ask for assist right now. Instead, spend 15 minutes looking for to resolve the problem. But if you can't repair it, you could now ask for help.

But earlier than asking all and sundry's help, you want to listing down the "bits and portions" of the problem. Specify what you already did and what region you possibly did not able to remedy.

This system will assist the helper to determine out the trouble and make effective movements.

If you are given a undertaking on that you don't realise what to do, try to do it through yourself first. Make an internet studies. Read references and exceptional materials that allow you to continue.

Conclusion

We arrived at the end of this Book. If we make a short summary, we are capable to mention that we've got were given found out masses about the manner to gaining knowledge of your highbrow popularity. We have observed that hobby is the system thru which we pick out out some stimulus from our surroundings, this is, we cognizance on a stimulus and forget approximately all others that aren't applicable to us.

Also, we've got got were given observed out that interest is composed in voluntarily centering all the attention of the mind on an aim, item or hobby this is being carried out or considering performing at that moment, for a long term leaving apart the complete series of events or distinct gadgets that can be able to interfere of their fulfillment or of their hobby.

There is not any doubt that hobby is best accessed from highbrow calm. And intellectual calm is handiest accessed from rest. That way that it is critical to find calm while making selections.

To understand this concept, we must go through in mind that this practice is not a modern-day-day invention, but moreover it has its foundations in meditation. And meditating is a very wholesome addiction for personnel, managers, specialists, humans, who need to lessen their pressure ranges. The attention and master of the mental focus emerge as a tool to apply for those advantages in a realistic way to regular lifestyles, every professionally and for my part.

Stop, learn how to prevent to get higher the calm and with it the attention, it supposes to take the selection to do it. Relaxing is an paintings, a manner. And it is critical to study it. This can be a subject that all productiveness professionals should hold close.